I0571457

THE PRACTICAL GUIDE TO FAMILY PREPAREDNESS

EASY, SIMPLE, AND COST-EFFECTIVE STRATEGIES FOR EVERY HOME TO ENSURE PEACE OF MIND DURING A CRISIS

SCOTT C. PYRON

© **Copyright 2024 - All rights reserved.**

The content contained within this book may not be reproduced, duplicated or transmitted without direct written permission from the author or the publisher.

Under no circumstances will any blame or legal responsibility be held against the publisher, or author, for any damages, reparation, or monetary loss due to the information contained within this book, either directly or indirectly.

Legal Notice:

This book is copyright protected. It is only for personal use. You cannot amend, distribute, sell, use, quote or paraphrase any part, or the content within this book, without the consent of the author or publisher.

Disclaimer Notice:

Please note the information contained within this document is for educational and entertainment purposes only. All effort has been executed to present accurate, up to date, reliable, complete information. No warranties of any kind are declared or implied. Readers acknowledge that the author is not engaged in the rendering of legal, financial, medical or professional advice. The content within this book has been derived from various sources. Please consult a licensed professional before attempting any techniques outlined in this book.

By reading this document, the reader agrees that under no circumstances is the author responsible for any losses, direct or indirect, that are incurred as a result of the use of the information contained within this document, including, but not limited to, errors, omissions, or inaccuracies.

CONTENTS

To the man, I can only hope to be one day. I love you, Dad!

The just man walketh in his integrity: his children are blessed after him.

— PROVERBS 20:7 (KJV)

INTRODUCTION

In life, wisdom often lies in foresight and preparation. As Proverbs 22:3 wisely states, "A prudent man foreseeth the evil, and hideth himself: but the simple pass on, and are punished" (*King James Bible*, 2023b). This biblical verse underscores the importance of being proactive and taking steps to protect our families.

Consider this scenario: If a disaster were to strike unexpectedly, would you and your family be prepared? It's a question that may not cross your mind daily, yet the actions taken in those initial moments of an emergency could be critical for survival.

Take, for example, the story of Karen and Kevin. Like many families, they never anticipated facing a life-altering event. However, when a sudden storm wreaked havoc in their neighborhood, their lack of preparation became glaringly evident. Without a plan in place, they found themselves scrambling to ensure their family's safety amid the chaos.

Statistics reveal a sobering reality—only 39% of Americans have developed an emergency plan and discussed it with their families ("Infographic: Prepare for Everywhere," 2024). This alarming statistic underscores the urgent need for readiness and preparedness in every household.

As you reflect on your own family's preparedness, you may recognize the importance of taking proactive steps to safeguard your loved ones. Whether prompted by recent natural disasters, personal experiences, or a desire to ensure your family's well-being, the catalyst for seeking out resources on emergency preparedness is often deeply personal.

In today's unpredictable world, the significance of readiness and preparedness cannot be overstated, particularly for the whole family. It's not just about having a plan in place; it's about equipping ourselves with the knowledge and resources to navigate emergencies with confidence and resilience. Throughout this book, we will explore practical strategies and expert insights to help you and your family become better prepared for whatever challenges may lie ahead. So, let's embark on this journey together as we prioritize the safety and security of those we hold dear.

In addition to preparedness, adaptability plays a crucial role in facing unexpected challenges. As highlighted in a study published in ScienceDirect, adaptability enables individuals to navigate unforeseen circumstances effectively, ultimately enhancing their ability to respond and recover from emergencies (Nursetiawati et al., 2023).

Take, for instance, Nancy's story. Despite facing a devastating flood, Nancy's family emerged unscathed thanks to their meticulous emergency planning. Similarly, Zoe and Kelly's stories underscore the life-saving impact of preparedness in the face of adversity.

Throughout this book, you'll gain invaluable shortcuts to preparedness. From comprehensive emergency plans to the practical stockpiling of insights and adaptability strategies, each chapter provides actionable advice to streamline your preparedness journey, helping you gain a transformed outlook on emergency preparedness. You'll gain the confidence and skills to safeguard your family's well-being, ensuring peace of mind in any situation.

I've been where you are right now, not knowing where to start, so I decided to bring years of experience in emergency planning and response to this book. Having navigated my own family through various crises, I understand the challenges and importance of readiness firsthand.

Before delving into Chapter 1, take a moment to assess your current state of preparedness with the self-assessment questionnaire provided. This will serve as a valuable benchmark as you embark on your journey toward greater readiness and security.

SELF-ASSESSMENT QUESTIONNAIRE: EVALUATING YOUR PREPAREDNESS

1. Emergency Communication

A. Do you have a designated meeting place and communication plan in case your family is separated during an emergency?
B. Have you exchanged contact information with family members, neighbors, and emergency contacts?
C. Are you familiar with local emergency broadcast channels and communication methods during disasters?

2. Emergency Supplies

A. Do you have a stocked emergency kit containing essential items, such as non-perishable food, water, medications, first aid supplies, a flashlight, and batteries?
B. Are your emergency supplies regularly checked and replenished to ensure they are up-to-date and functional?
C. Do you have specialized supplies for family members with unique needs, such as infants, elderly members, or pets?

3. Home Safety Measures

A. Does your home have smoke detectors, carbon monoxide detectors, and fire extinguishers?
B. Are heavy furniture and appliances secured to prevent injuries during earthquakes or other disasters?
C. Do you know how to shut off utilities like gas, water, and electricity in case of emergencies?

4. Financial Preparedness

A. Do you have an emergency fund to cover unexpected expenses during a crisis?
B. Do you have adequate insurance coverage for your home, health, and belongings to mitigate financial risks?
C. Have you developed a budgeting plan to ensure financial stability during emergencies?

5. Emergency Drills and Training

A. Do you conduct regular emergency drills with your family to practice evacuation procedures and safety protocols?
B. Have you received training in CPR, first aid, and other life-saving techniques?
C. Are you familiar with the emergency plans and procedures at your workplace, children's schools, and other frequented locations?

6. Community Resources and Support

A. Are you aware of local emergency shelters, hospitals, and evacuation routes in your area?
B. Do you participate in community preparedness initiatives or organizations to stay informed and connected?
C. Are you familiar with community resources and support services available during emergencies, such as emergency hotlines or disaster relief programs?

7. Emotional and Psychological Preparedness

A. Do you have strategies in place to cope with stress, anxiety, or trauma during emergencies?
B. Have you discussed emergency preparedness and safety measures with your family to alleviate fears and uncertainties?
C. Are you proactive in maintaining mental and emotional well-being through self-care practices and support networks?

8. Documentation and Important Records

A. Have you organized and secured important documents such as identification, insurance policies, and medical records in waterproof and fireproof containers?
B. Do you have digital copies of essential documents stored securely online or in cloud storage for easy access during emergencies?
C. Have you communicated the location of important documents and emergency plans to trusted family members or contacts?

9. Special Considerations

A. Do you have contingency plans for specific scenarios, such as power outages, severe weather events, or medical emergencies?
B. Have you considered the needs of family members with disabilities, medical conditions, or mobility limitations in your emergency planning?
C. Are you prepared to adapt your emergency plans and strategies based on changing circumstances and evolving risks?

Scoring

Every "Yes" answer equals one point. Assign one point for each "Yes" response.

Total your points to assess your current level of preparedness:

- 0–3 points: Low preparedness; significant improvements needed.
- 4–6 points: Moderate preparedness; room for enhancement.
- 7–9 points: High preparedness; well-prepared with some areas for refinement.
- 10–12 points: Excellent preparedness; comprehensive readiness with minimal gaps.

CULTIVATING A PREPAREDNESS MINDSET

 If thou faint in the day of adversity, thy strength is small.

— PROVERBS 24:10 (KJV)

This biblical counsel encourages us to stand resilient in challenging situations, emphasizing that real strength is demonstrated by enduring difficulties. Essentially, it suggests that the ability to withstand and overcome trials speaks to one's inner fortitude.

Interestingly, post-emergency statistical data paints an encouraging picture of human resilience. Studies show that over 80% of individuals affected by challenging events recover well, without enduring prolonged distress that significantly impacts their mental health ("Preparing Emotionally for Disasters and Emergencies," 2024). This statistic shows us people's inherent capacity to bounce back and regain a sense of well-being after facing adversity.

This impressive percentage also highlights the human ability to adapt, cope, and recover, showcasing strength even amid adversity. It also underscores the importance of nurturing resilience as a vital aspect of mental health and overall well-being.

As we navigate life's uncertainties, these biblical and statistical insights intertwine, reminding us of the enduring human spirit. The verse prompts contemplation on our inner strength during tough times, while the statistics offer concrete evidence of the widespread ability to recover and emerge stronger from adversity. Together, they tell a story of hope and resilience, inspiring us to confront difficulties with fortitude and courage.

UNDERSTANDING MENTAL AND EMOTIONAL READINESS

Emotional readiness isn't merely about being unshaken by adversity; it's about possessing foundational emotional skills to flourish in the face of challenges. At its core lies resilience—the capacity to navigate life's trials while discovering pathways to thrive.

While physical preparedness garners significant attention, the importance of mental and emotional readiness is equally profound. Being mentally prepared equips you to navigate the emotional turbulence of emergencies, fostering a sense of stability and clarity amid chaos.

Emotional preparedness goes beyond a stoic response to difficulties. It involves possessing foundational emotional skills that serve as the cornerstone of psychological well-being. These are skills such as self-awareness, self-regulation, empathy, and effective interpersonal communication. At its essence, emotional preparedness revolves around resilience—the dynamic capacity to navigate life's trials and tribulations. Resilience isn't just about bouncing back; it's about bouncing forward, discovering new paths, and thriving in the face of adversity. It's the ability to view any challenge as an opportunity to learn and grow.

Emotional or mental preparedness isn't just about surviving; it's about thriving. It's the intentional cultivation of a mindset that doesn't just weather the storm but learns to dance in the rain. Flourishing amid challenges involves tapping into emotional intelligence, fostering positive coping mechanisms, and embracing the inherent potential for growth within difficulties.

But how do we achieve this? How do we mentally prepare ourselves and our families for an emergency?

There is a simple framework you can use: Anticipate, identify, and manage—or as I like to call it: AIM. This three-step framework is a powerful guide not only for preparing for an emergency but also for navigating the rough waters during a crisis.

Anticipate: Proactive Insight Into Stress Responses

Anticipation entails simply peering into the future, albeit in a psychological context. It prompts us to reflect and project how we might react under the stress of an emergency. You need to take a deep dive into self-awareness, considering your emotional and cognitive responses when faced with heightened stress. This will allow you to identify potential emotional triggers and vulnerabilities.

Armed with this foresight, a comprehensive preparedness plan can be crafted. For instance, knowing that certain stressors may induce anxiety enables one to include anxiety management strategies in their emergency preparedness toolkit.

During an emergency, the foresight gained through anticipation becomes a guiding light. You can recognize the early signs of stress, enabling the swift initiation of coping mechanisms. This proactive approach prevents emotional escalation and aids in maintaining a composed and adaptive demeanor in the face of a crisis.

Identify: Recognizing Emotional Landscapes

Identification involves recognizing and understanding the intricate landscape of thoughts and feelings that arise during challenging times. It's a process of introspection that unveils the patterns of emotional responses, offering insights into both cognitive and affective reactions.

Understanding your emotional landscape equips you with a nuanced map of your emotional responses. This knowledge becomes instrumental in crafting a tailored emergency preparedness plan. For instance, recognizing a tendency to feel overwhelmed allows the inclusion of relaxation techniques in the preparedness strategy.

In the heat of an emergency, the ability to identify your emotions in real time is invaluable. This self-awareness facilitates swift decision-making and adaptive responses. Recognizing the emotional terrain allows for effective management, preventing the onset of panic and helping to foster a focused mindset.

Manage: Applying Proactive Coping Strategies

Management is the final phase where proactive coping strategies are developed to navigate increased stress. This involves formulating a plan detailing how you will respond to elevated stress levels, ensuring a composed and resilient approach. Crafting effective coping mechanisms is a crucial aspect of preparedness. To help you develop coping strategies, you can learn relaxation techniques and mindfulness practices, or seek support from others. The preparedness plan becomes a personalized toolkit for managing stress and enhancing overall resilience.

During an emergency, the ability to manage heightened stress is paramount. The coping strategies, diligently prepared in advance, become the pillars of emotional fortitude. Whether it's deep breathing exercises, positive affirmations, or seeking social support, the management phase ensures a proactive response to stressors.

The AIM framework offers a dynamic and proactive approach to emergency preparedness. By incorporating self-awareness, emotional intelligence, and targeted coping strategies, you not only equip yourself for potential challenges but also navigate emergencies with resilience, composure, and adaptability. This framework is a versatile tool—a mental compass that guides us through the storm and helps us emerge stronger on the other side.

When stress looms and the unforeseen occurs, a calm and collected mental state becomes a vital asset. During an emergency, maintaining composure enables clear-headed thinking and swift decision-making. Cultivating a calm mind is instrumental in crisis management. It fosters the ability to think rationally, act decisively, and serve as a stabilizing force for those around you—a leadership quality that is crucial in emergencies.

Life is unpredictable, and emergencies often unfold without warning. Mental readiness equips you with the invaluable skill of adaptability. Flexibility in adjusting plans and strategies becomes a defining trait when confronted with unforeseen challenges, and the ability to adapt is synonymous with an effective emergency response. Rigidity can lead to setbacks, but mental readiness ensures a nimble approach, facilitating quick adjustments and innovative problem-solving during critical moments.

While mental readiness begins at an individual level, its true potency manifests when embraced collectively. A community, family, or team that shares a commitment to mental preparedness becomes a resilient force, capable of withstanding the trials of an emergency.

The aftermath of an emergency demands not only survival but also a swift and robust recovery. Those who approach emergencies with mental readiness recover more efficiently, laying the groundwork for a stronger and more enduring restoration.

The positive correlation between mental readiness and effective emergency response is a serious consideration. It involves maintaining composure, fostering adaptability, building collective resilience, and ensuring a prompt and resilient recovery. Embrace the gravity of mental preparedness—it stands as a foundational element in facing the unpredictable nature of life's challenges.

BUILDING RESILIENCE IN YOURSELF AND YOUR FAMILY

In the face of crisis, adopting a disaster resilience mindset isn't just an option; it's your key to conquering the challenges of the unexpected. Let's cut through the jargon and get real about resilience. It's not just a fancy term; it's your ticket to swiftly getting back to normal life after chaos hits. Think of it as your secret sauce—flexibility and resistance bundled up for a rapid recovery post-catastrophe.

Disaster resilience isn't a one-size-fits-all deal. It's about flexing and adapting when everything around you is in chaos. No sitting around waiting; it's about being dynamic, making quick adjustments, and facing unpredictable challenges head-on. Resilience isn't about enduring hardships; it's a proactive stance against the disaster's negative impacts—picture not just surviving but efficiently restoring all functions. It's not just weathering the storm; it's about thriving in its aftermath.

Disaster resilience isn't a spectator sport. It's the MVP in efficient post-crisis recovery with a swift rebound where the restored normalcy minimizes the disaster's long-term impacts. It's all about proactive anticipation, planning, and always being a step ahead.

Communities, families, and individuals armed with resilience are the A-Team in facing unexpected events. They're not just weathering the storm; they're outsmarting it. Enhanced resilience means anticipating disasters better, planning more effectively, and ultimately reducing losses.

It's not about twiddling thumbs and hoping for the best. It's about taking charge, planning, and strategizing for potential disasters before they unfold. It's not a concept; it's your dynamic approach to crisis management, ensuring not just survival but the speedy revival of all functions.

As we navigate the chaos of disasters, understanding and building resilience become our power move. Remember, resilience is not something that happens overnight, and it's not just a natural trademark for the hero. It's your indispensable strategy for a robust response and recovery that can be cultivated. Here are 12 key factors for building disaster resilience in yourself and your family:

1. Open Dialogue

Start by fostering open communication. Build a foundation of trust by encouraging family members to share their thoughts, feelings, and concerns which is essential for resilience.

2. Learn and Grow

Embrace the mindset of continuous learning. Treat challenges as opportunities for growth. Instill in your family the belief that every obstacle is a chance to learn, adapt, and emerge stronger.

3. Establish Routines

A routine provides stability, so create daily routines for your family, especially during turbulent times. Predictability in daily life helps reduce stress and fosters a sense of security.

4. Encourage Problem-Solving

Teach problem-solving skills to your family members, where instead of focusing on the problem, guide them to explore solutions. This empowers them to face challenges with a proactive approach.

5. Promote Flexibility

Resilience thrives on adaptability. Teach your family the art of flexibility—the ability to adjust and pivot when situations change. This skill is invaluable in navigating the unexpected.

6. Build a Support System

Resilience is often a group effort. Cultivate a strong support system within your family, by encouraging them to lean on each other for strength during tough times.

7. Mindfulness and Coping Strategies

Introduce mindfulness and stress-reducing techniques. Whether it's deep breathing, meditation, or other coping mechanisms, these practices equip your family with tools to manage stress effectively.

8. Celebrate Achievements

Acknowledge and celebrate both small and big achievements. This fosters a positive atmosphere, reinforcing the idea that overcoming challenges is not only possible but worthy of recognition.

9. Teach Self-Compassion

Help your family understand that setbacks are a part of life. Teach them self-compassion, emphasizing the importance of treating oneself with kindness and understanding during difficult times.

10. Lead by Example

Your actions speak louder than words, so demonstrate resilience in your own life. Show your family how to face challenges with a positive attitude, determination, and a belief in their ability to overcome hardships.

11. Encourage Social Connections

Strong social ties are a pillar of resilience. Foster connections within your family and encourage relationships with friends and extended family. Social support is a powerful buffer against stress.

12. Cultivate Optimism

Foster an optimistic outlook on life, by encouraging your family to focus on positive aspects, even in challenging situations. Optimism fuels resilience and helps maintain a hopeful perspective.

Remember, building resilience is an ongoing process. By incorporating these strategies into your family's daily life, you're not just preparing for challenges, you're fortifying your family to thrive in the face of adversity.

Maintaining Positivity and Practicing Stress-Relief Techniques

In the rollercoaster of life, maintaining a positive outlook and incorporating stress-relief techniques are not just luxuries; they are essential tools for a resilient and thriving existence. Let's delve into why these aspects hold such profound importance:

Maintaining a Positive Outlook

Positivity serves as a shield for your mental well-being. When facing challenges, maintaining a positive outlook fosters mental resilience, helping you navigate difficulties with a clearer and more focused mind. It also contributes to emotional stability, allowing you to manage stress, anxiety, and other emotional challenges more effectively. This helps foster a sense of calm and balance. Studies consistently show that a positive mindset correlates with better physical health it can enhance your immune system, reduce the risk of chronic diseases, and contribute to an overall healthier lifestyle (Corliss, 2020).

Positivity fuels creativity and enhances problem-solving skills. When faced with obstacles, a positive mindset enables you to approach issues with optimism, finding innovative solutions more readily. A positive demeanor is infectious; it not only benefits you but also positively influences those around you. Healthy relationships are built on optimism, understanding, and the ability to navigate challenges together.

Stress-Relief Techniques

Chronic stress can take a toll on your physical health. Stress-relief techniques, such as exercise, deep breathing, or meditation, contribute to overall well-being by reducing the physiological impact of stress on the body. By engaging in activities that alleviate stress, you create a healthier emotional balance, preventing emotional overload.

Stress can also cloud your mind and impede productivity. Incorporating stress-relief techniques helps clear mental fog, allowing for improved focus, concentration, and overall productivity.

Ultimately, practicing stress-relief techniques enhances your overall quality of life. By managing stress effectively, you create a foundation for a more enjoyable and fulfilling existence.

1. Deep Breathing

Technique: Inhale deeply for a count of four, hold your breath for four counts, and exhale slowly for another four counts.

Why It Works: Deep breathing activates the body's relaxation response, reducing stress and promoting calmness.

2. Grounding Exercises

Technique: Focus on your senses. Identify five things you can see, four things you can touch, three things you can hear, two things you can smell, and one thing you can taste.

Why It Works: Grounding brings attention to the present moment, diverting your mind from stressors.

3. Mindful Walking

Technique: Take slow, deliberate steps, paying attention to each movement. Focus on your breath and the sensation of your feet on the ground.

Why It Works: Mindful walking combines physical activity with mindfulness, promoting relaxation.

4. Positive Visualization

Technique: Close your eyes and imagine a place or scenario that brings you peace and joy. Picture the details vividly.

Why It Works: Positive visualization counteracts stress by redirecting your thoughts to a calming mental image.

5. Progressive Muscle Relaxation

Technique: Tense and then gradually release each muscle group, starting from your toes and working up to your head.

Why It Works: Progressive muscle relaxation helps release physical tension and induces a state of relaxation.

6. Journaling

Technique: Write down your thoughts and feelings. Documenting your experiences can help process emotions and reduce stress.

Why It Works: Journaling provides an outlet for expression and reflection.

7. Crisis Coping Statements

Technique: Develop positive and reassuring phrases like "I can handle this," or "I am resilient," and repeat them during moments of stress.

Why It Works: Coping statements affirm your ability to manage challenging situations.

8. Connect With Others

Technique: Reach out to friends, family, or support groups. Share your feelings and seek comfort in social connections.

Why It Works: Social support is a powerful stress buffer, fostering a sense of community and understanding.

9. Prayer or Meditation

Technique: Engage in prayer or meditation practices that align with your beliefs.

Why It Works: Spiritual practices can provide solace and a sense of connection to something greater.

10. Emergency Kit Mindfulness Objects

Technique: Pack a small item in your emergency kit that brings you comfort or has sentimental value. Use it as a mindfulness anchor during stressful times.

Why It Works: Having a tangible reminder of positivity can provide emotional support.

Remember, the key is to practice these techniques regularly so that they become familiar and effective in times of stress. Customize them to suit your preferences and include them as part of your emergency preparedness plan.

CREATING RESILIENT FAMILY HABITS

Building resilience within your family is no longer an option—it's a must. Life throws challenges our way, but a resilient family is one that not only weathers the storm but comes out stronger on the other side. Let's delve into the key habits of highly resilient families and practical tips on involving everyone, especially the kids, in fostering this resilience.

1. Create a list of family values and rules. Start by sitting down as a family and hammering out your core values and rules. What matters to each member? What are the non-negotiables? This sets the groundwork for facing any challenge that comes your way.
2. Be nurturing and speak your family's love languages. Love is what holds us together, so take the time to figure out each family member's love language and speak it. It could be words of affirmation, acts of service, or quality time; tailor your expressions of love to each individual.
3. Collect positive memories and build your family's emotional bank. Every family has a unique collection of positive memories. Whether it's a camping trip, a cozy movie night, or celebrating achievements, cherish these moments. Regularly revisit them to reinforce a sense of togetherness.
4. Demonstrate how to adapt and be flexible in different situations. Life is unpredictable, and adaptability is a superpower. Share stories of times when being flexible led

to positive outcomes. Teach your kids the art of adapting to change with resilience.

5. Make problem-solving a family exercise. When challenges arise, tackle them together. Involve everyone in problem-solving. This collaborative approach not only resolves issues but also teaches your children valuable life skills.

6. Don't be shy to ask for help. Strength lies in seeking support when needed, so foster an environment where asking for help is encouraged. This teaches your family that they're not alone and that supporting each other is crucial.

7. Make time to rejuvenate and recharge. Life can be hectic, but family downtime is non-negotiable. Whether it's a lazy Sunday afternoon, a family movie night, or a weekend outing, allocate time for relaxation and rejuvenation.

Family meetings should be the norm. Encourage open communication, providing a platform for everyone to share their thoughts and feelings. Make resilience-building relatable and engaging for everyone involved by adjusting discussions and activities to the age of each family member. Collaborative projects are a great way to strengthen family bonds. Whether it's tending to a garden, embarking on a DIY home project, or planning a special event, working together fosters unity.

Storytelling is a powerful tool. Share family stories, including challenges and how they were overcome. This helps children understand that setbacks are a natural part of life. Also, cultivate a culture of appreciation for each other, and discuss positive aspects of challenging situations; expressing gratitude should be a regular practice.

Introduce mindfulness activities suitable for different ages. Guided meditation, deep breathing exercises, or nature walks can contribute to a calmer, more resilient family. Encourage decision-making based on age appropriateness. Involving children in decision-making processes fosters a sense of responsibility and autonomy.

By integrating these habits and involving your family in resilience-building activities, you're not just weathering the storm; you're turning challenges into opportunities for growth. It's time to build a family that doesn't just survive but thrives in the face of adversity.

Winston Churchill once said, "Success is not final, failure is not fatal: It is the courage to continue that counts" ("A Quote By Winston S. Churchill," n.d). These words echo the enduring spirit of resilience, emphasizing that setbacks do not define us; it's the persistence and courage to persevere through challenges that truly matter.

ESSENTIALS OF AN EMERGENCY KIT

 By failing to prepare, you are preparing to fail.

— BENJAMIN FRANKLIN

I n the face of uncertainties, preparation is not just a choice but a decisive action that can make the difference between chaos and control. This chapter is your guide to building a comprehensive emergency kit—a crucial step toward ensuring the safety and well-being of your family. Before we dive into all the hows, whys, and whats of an emergency kit, we first need to know what an emergency kit is.

An emergency kit is a collection of essential items and supplies that are crucial to have on hand in the event of unexpected disasters or emergencies. The primary purpose of an emergency kit is to provide individuals and families with the necessary resources to sustain themselves for at least 72 hours when regular services may be disrupted.

In times of crisis, you might find yourself without access to power, tap water, or immediate assistance. Hence, being self-sufficient for at least 72 hours becomes vital. This duration allows for a buffer period during which emergency services can mobilize and regular utilities can be restored.

The need for an emergency kit becomes particularly apparent in situations where evacuation is necessary, such as during natural disasters like floodwaters, earthquakes, tornados, severe storms, wildfires, or even man-made threats. In these cases, having a well-prepared emergency kit (also referred to as a bug-out bag or a go-bag) ensures that you can quickly grab essential items and evacuate (bug-out) to a safer location, minimizing the risks associated with the disaster.

Similarly, an emergency kit is invaluable if you find yourself stranded inside your home (bug-in) without the ability to receive assistance for an extended period. Whether due to severe weather conditions, power outages, or social unrest, having a well-stocked kit ensures that you have the necessary supplies to sustain yourself and your family until help arrives or normal services are restored.

In essence, an emergency kit is a proactive measure to ensure that you and your loved ones are not caught off guard during unexpected events, providing a sense of security and self-sufficiency during challenging times.

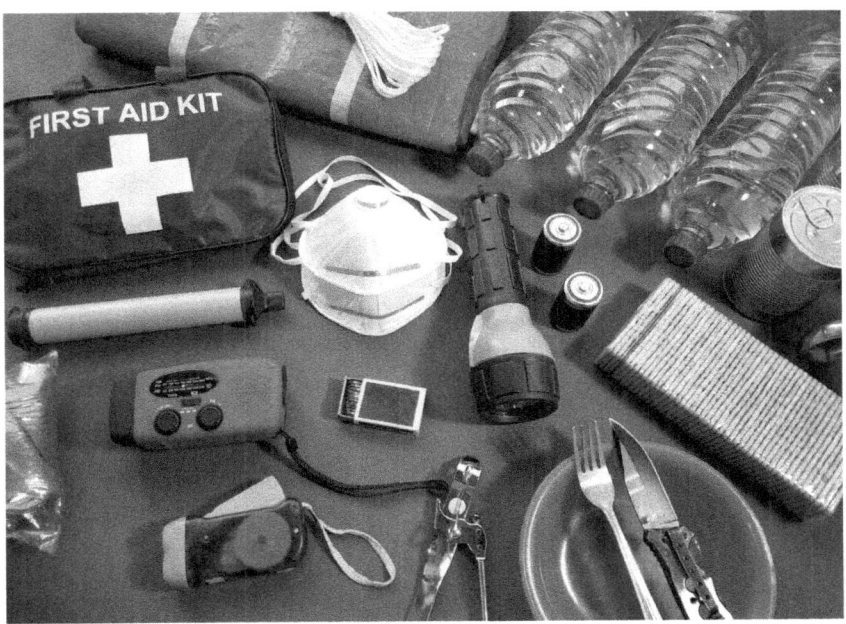

COMPREHENSIVE LIST OF EMERGENCY KIT ITEMS

Creating a comprehensive emergency kit is a crucial step in ensuring you're well-prepared for unexpected situations. Here's a detailed guide to help you assemble your emergency kit:

Step 1: Choosing a Container

Choosing the right container for your emergency kit is a critical first step to ensure that your supplies are well-organized, easily transportable, and protected. Here are some of the options you can consider:

Sturdy Backpack:

- They are portable and hands-free, allowing for easy mobility during evacuations.
- They have multiple compartments that provide organization for different types of items.
- Some backpacks come with built-in hydration systems.
- Ensure it's made of durable, water-resistant material.
- Opt for padded shoulder straps for comfort during extended wear.

Waterproof Storage Bin:

- These bins provide excellent protection as their designed to keep out water and moisture.
- It can be a more substantial option, accommodating a larger quantity of supplies.
- It is helpful to find one that is stackable and easy to store in a designated area.
- Choose a bin with a secure, airtight seal to prevent water ingress.
- Ensure it's made of robust materials to withstand impact.

Dedicated Emergency Kit Bag:

- They are designed specifically for emergency preparedness, often with multiple compartments.
- Some bags come with reflective strips for visibility in low light.
- The bags are usually made from durable and weather-resistant materials.
- Look for a bag with reinforced stitching for added durability.

- Check for adjustable straps for comfortable carrying.

Rolling Duffel Bag:

- They combine the portability of a backpack with the convenience of wheels.
- They are suitable for individuals who may struggle to carry a backpack for an extended period.
- They offer a substantial amount of storage space.
- Ensure the wheels are sturdy and can handle various terrains.
- Buy a bag that is equipped with both handles and shoulder straps for versatile carrying options.

Tactical or Military-Style Bag:

- They are designed for rugged use and often include modular lightweight load-carrying equipment (MOLLE) and customizable webbing.
- They are durable and may offer additional features like hydration compatibility.
- These tactical bags come in various shapes and sizes for different needs.
- Ensure it's comfortable to carry for extended periods.
- Check for reinforced stitching and quality zippers.

Ultimately, the choice of container depends on your personal preferences, the size of your family, and the specific needs of your emergency kit. Consider factors like mobility, storage space, and protection against the elements when making your selection.

Step 2: Food for Energy and Sustenance

When selecting non-perishable food items for your emergency kit, it's crucial to prioritize energy-dense and high-caloric options with a long shelf life. During times of immense stress, we burn calories much faster than normal, so stocking up on high-calorie food is vital for your and your family's survival. Here are more details on the types of foods to include and considerations for ensuring your nutritional needs are met during an emergency:

Energy Bars:

- They are compact and lightweight, making them easy to pack.
- Typically, they are designed to provide a quick energy boost.
- They come in various flavors and formulations, including those with added protein and vitamins.
- Regularly check the expiration date and rotate stock.
- Be mindful of any allergies or dietary restrictions among family members.

Canned Goods:

- They are durable and resistant to environmental factors.
- They can include a variety of options, such as fruits, vegetables, meats, and soups.
- Many canned items can be eaten directly from the can, eliminating the need for cooking.
- Opt for cans with pop-top lids for convenience.
- Ensure a manual can opener is included in your kit if necessary.

Dried Fruits:

- They are lightweight and space-efficient.
- They provide natural sugars for a quick energy boost.
- They can be a good source of essential vitamins and minerals.
- Choose options without added sugars or preservatives.
- Pack them in airtight containers to maintain freshness.

Nut and Seed Mixes:

- They are high in healthy fats, protein, and essential nutrients.
- They provide sustained energy over an extended period.
- They come in various combinations, including trail mixes and nut bars.
- Be mindful of potential allergies, especially for nut-containing mixes.
- Ensure the packaging is resealable for extended freshness.

Liquid Meals (Meal Replacement Shakes):

- They are convenient and ready to drink.
- They are often formulated to provide a balanced nutritional profile.
- They can serve as a quick and complete meal substitute.
- Check the expiration date and replace them as needed.
- Consider individual preferences and dietary needs.

Instant Oatmeal or Cereal Cups:

- They are quick and easy to prepare with minimal water requirements.
- They often come in single-serving cups for convenience.
- They provide a source of carbohydrates for sustained energy.
- Include a portable stove or water heating method in your kit.
- Choose varieties with added nutrients.

Peanut Butter or Nut Butter Packets:

- They boast rich levels of beneficial fats and protein.
- Single portions reduce waste and guarantee freshness.
- These items are adaptable and can be spread on crackers or enjoyed by themselves.
- Remember to check for any allergies among family members.
- Opt for packets to avoid the need for a knife.

Hardtack or Crackers:

- They have a long shelf life and are moisture-resistant.
- They serve as a base for spreads like peanut butter or cheese.
- They are compact and easy to portion.
- Ensure they are stored in airtight containers to prevent staleness.
- Take into account flavor preferences and dietary restrictions.

Don't forget to routinely inspect the expiration dates of the food items in your emergency kit and replace any nearing their limits. Additionally, consider the specific dietary needs and preferences of your family members to ensure the kit meets everyone's requirements.

Step 3: Water

In general, it is recommended that you have a minimum of one gallon of water per person per day for at least three days. For optimum preparedness, consider aiming for a two-week supply if feasible. When choosing containers, prioritize compact and portable options for easy transportation, such as collapsible water containers, water pouches, or sturdy water bottles. The portability of these containers becomes particularly crucial if evacuation becomes necessary.

Opt for containers crafted from dark or opaque materials to prevent sunlight from fostering algae growth. It is imperative to guarantee that the containers boast a secure, airtight seal to thwart contamination. Select containers that are both explicitly designed for storing drinking water and clearly labeled as food-grade.

Maintain the freshness of your water supply by implementing a regular rotation schedule, with a recommended replacement every six months. Clearly label containers with the date of filling to facilitate efficient tracking of rotation.

For accessibility and convenience, store water containers in a designated and easily reachable location. Be acquainted with the emergency shut-off valves for water in your home. Uphold hygienic practices by regularly cleaning and sanitizing water containers to prevent bacterial growth. Additionally, include hand sanitizer or sanitizing wipes in your kit to ensure hygiene maintenance.

Here are some additional considerations you may want to remember:

- Include water purification tablets or drops in your kit to treat water from unfamiliar sources if needed.
- Consider compact water filtration devices as an additional layer of protection, especially if you may need to source water from natural bodies like rivers or lakes.
- Factor in water requirements not only for drinking but also for hygiene and cooking.

- Consider the needs of children and pets in your household when calculating water requirements.
- In some situations, you may be able to collect rainwater. As a result, include a rainwater collection system or appropriate containers in your emergency supplies.
- Identify nearby natural water sources, but be prepared to purify or filter the water before consumption.

Remember, water is essential not only for drinking but also for personal hygiene and food preparation. Being prepared with a sufficient and accessible water supply is a fundamental aspect of any well-rounded emergency kit.

Step 4: Shelter and Warmth

Pack lightweight and compact items for shelter, such as a Mylar emergency blanket, a tent, or a tarp. Additionally, include warm clothing, hats, and gloves to protect against the elements.

Mylar Emergency Blanket:

- These blankets are lightweight, compact, and excellent for retaining body heat.
- These reflective blankets are designed to provide insulation and are particularly effective in preventing heat loss.
- Ensure you have an adequate number for each person in your household.

Tent or Tarp:

- Include a lightweight and easily portable tent or tarp.
- These items can offer more substantial shelter and protection from the elements.
- Choose a tent that is quick to set up and suitable for your family size.
- Alternatively, a durable tarp can be used to create a makeshift shelter when needed.

Warm Clothing:

- Pack extra layers of warm clothing for each family member.
- Consider the climate of your region, and include items such as thermal underwear, insulated jackets, and waterproof outer layers.
- Don't forget to include hats and gloves to provide comprehensive protection against cold weather.

Emergency Sleeping Bag:

- In addition to the Mylar blankets, consider adding emergency sleeping bags to your kit.
- These compact, lightweight bags are designed for insulation and can be crucial for maintaining body heat in challenging conditions.

Portable Heating Sources:

- While it may not be feasible to include large heating sources in your emergency kit, consider compact options, such as hand warmers or portable camping stoves.

- These can provide a source of warmth in a controlled manner.

Emergency Shelter Guidelines:

- Include a set of guidelines or instructions on how to set up an emergency shelter using the items in your kit.
- This can be helpful, especially if you are not familiar with assembling makeshift shelters.

Remember to regularly check and update the contents of your emergency kit, ensuring that all shelter and warmth items remain in good condition and are suitable for the current season.

Step 5: Cooking, Fuel, and Light

Include a portable camping stove or compact cooking tools that operate without electricity. Pack fuel canisters or other appropriate fuel sources. Also, bring a flashlight, headlamp, or lantern with extra batteries for illumination.

Portable Camping Stove:

- Choose a compact and portable camping stove that operates without electricity.
- Look for options that are lightweight and easy to use.
- Many camping stoves use propane or butane canisters, providing a reliable source of heat for cooking.
- Ensure the stove is in good working condition and includes any necessary attachments.

Compact Cooking Tools:

- Pack essential cooking tools that are versatile and space-saving.
- Consider items like a compact pot, pan, and utensils.
- Collapsible or foldable designs are excellent for optimizing space in your emergency kit.

Fuel Canisters:

- Include an adequate supply of fuel canisters compatible with your camping stove.
- Check the expiration dates on fuel canisters regularly, and replace them as needed.
- It's crucial to have enough fuel to sustain cooking throughout the emergency period.

Alternative Fuel Sources:

- While camping stoves are convenient, consider alternative fuel sources such as portable charcoal grills or fuel tablets.
- Having options allows flexibility based on your situation and the availability of different fuel sources.

Flashlights, Headlamps, or Lanterns:

- Include reliable lighting sources such as a flashlight, headlamp, or lantern.
- Choose LED models for their energy efficiency and longer battery life.
- Ensure you have spare batteries, and regularly check the functionality of your lighting devices.

Lighting Safety:

- Pack lighting options with safety features such as adjustable brightness settings and durable, shatterproof casings.
- Hands-free lights such as headlamps can come in handy when you need both hands for a specific task.

Multi-Tool or Swiss Army Knife:

- Include a versatile multi-tool or Swiss Army knife in your kit.
- These tools often have built-in can openers, bottle openers, and other functionalities that can be invaluable during emergencies.

Cooking and Lighting Guidelines

- Provide simple instructions on how to safely use the cooking tools and lighting devices in your kit.
- Include tips on conserving fuel and extending battery life.

Step 6: Equipment and Tools

Essential tools include a multi-tool, a Swiss Army knife, duct tape, and a manual can opener. These versatile items can prove invaluable in various situations.

Multi-Tool:

- Choose a high-quality multi-tool with a variety of functions, such as pliers, screwdrivers, scissors, and a knife.

- Look for a compact and lightweight design for easy portability.
- Verify that all components of the multi-tool are in good working condition.

Swiss Army Knife:

- This is a versatile tool that typically includes a variety of blades, screwdrivers, can openers, and other functions.
- Select a Swiss Army knife with features that align with your potential needs during an emergency.
- Regularly check and lubricate moving parts to ensure smooth functionality.

Duct Tape:

- Duct tape is a versatile and durable adhesive tool that can be used for quick repairs, sealing, and securing items.
- Pack a roll of high-quality duct tape in your emergency kit.

Manual Can Opener:

- Include a manual can opener to access canned goods in your emergency food supply.
- Opt for a durable and rust-resistant can opener.
- Familiarize yourself with its operation, and ensure it is functional before adding it to your kit.

Additional Tools to Consider:

- Adjustable Wrench: Useful tool for tightening or loosening nuts and bolts.
- Screwdriver Set: Include a set with various head types and sizes.
- Hammer or Mallet: For tasks that require a bit more force.
- Small Saw or Wire Saw: Handy for cutting through materials in outdoor scenarios.
- Work Gloves: Protect your hands during manual tasks.

Having a well-rounded set of tools in your emergency kit ensures that you're prepared for a range of situations, from minor repairs to more complex tasks that may arise during an emergency.

Step 7: Personal Supplies and Medication

Don't forget to include personal hygiene items like toothbrushes, toothpaste, and sanitary supplies in your kit. Pack a basic first aid kit with essential medications, bandages, and any necessary prescription medications.

Personal Hygiene Items

Toothbrush and Toothpaste:

- Choose compact and travel-sized toothbrushes and toothpaste to save space.
- Consider including individual toothbrush covers for hygiene.

Sanitary Supplies:

- Include sanitary items such as sanitary pads or tampons for feminine hygiene.
- Pack wet wipes or tissues for personal cleanliness.

Hand Sanitizer:

- Include a small bottle of hand sanitizer to maintain hand hygiene.
- Opt for alcohol-based sanitizers with at least 60% alcohol content.

Basic First Aid Kit

Bandages and Dressings:

- Include an assortment of adhesive bandages in various sizes.
- Pack sterile gauze pads and adhesive dressings for wound care.

Antiseptic Wipes and Ointments:

- Include antiseptic wipes for cleaning wounds.
- Pack antibiotic ointment or cream to prevent infection.

Pain Relievers:

- Include over-the-counter pain relievers such as acetaminophen or ibuprofen.
- If applicable, include any prescription pain medications.

Allergy Medications:

- Include antihistamines for allergic reactions.
- If anyone in your family has specific allergies, ensure you have the necessary medications.

Prescription Medications:

- Pack a supply of essential prescription medications.
- Regularly check the expiration dates, and restock them as needed.

Medical Supplies:

- Include tweezers, scissors, and medical tape for minor medical procedures.
- Pack disposable gloves for hygiene and to protect against blood-borne pathogens.

Personalized Medical Information:

- Compile a list of each family member's allergies, medical conditions, and any pertinent medical history.
- Include emergency contact information for healthcare providers.

Regularly Check and Replace:

- Regularly inspect the contents of your first aid kit and replace any expired or used items.
- Consider storing medications in a separate, clearly labeled container to ease access.

Emergency Medications:

- If someone in the family requires specific emergency medications (e.g., epinephrine autoinjector like an Epi-pen, for severe allergies), ensure these are included.

Step 8: Personal Documents and Money

Keep copies of important documents like identification, insurance policies, and medical records in a waterproof container. Include some cash in small denominations as ATMs may not be accessible during emergencies.

Important Documents

Identification:

- Include photocopies of identification documents for each family member, such as passports, driver's licenses, and social security cards.
- If relevant, add copies of birth certificates and marriage certificates to your kit.

Insurance Policies:

- Make copies of insurance policies, including health, home, and auto insurance.
- Include contact information for insurance providers.

Medical Records:

- Include a summary of each family member's medical history and any essential medical records.
- Include information on allergies, medications, and past surgeries or medical procedures.

Property Documents:

- Include copies of property-related documents, such as deeds and rental agreements.
- If relevant, include proof of ownership for vehicles.

Financial Documents:

- Make sure to include copies of crucial financial documents, such as bank account information and

investment details, in your kit.
- Store information on outstanding loans or debts.

Choose a durable and waterproof container to safeguard documents from water damage. Consider using a sealable plastic bag or a waterproof pouch for added protection. Alternatively, you could make digital copies and save them on a USB drive, SD, hard drive, or even in the "Cloud." Place the container in a readily accessible location within your emergency kit.

Cash Reserves

Include a mix of small denominations and bills to facilitate transactions during emergencies. Aim for a sufficient amount to cover immediate needs, such as purchasing essential supplies. Remember that ATMs may be inaccessible during emergencies, making cash on hand crucial for transactions. It is also important to check and replenish the cash reserves to account for inflation and changing needs.

Emergency Contacts

Prepare a list of emergency contacts, including family members, close friends, and important service providers.

This emergency kit will ensure that you and your family are well-equipped to handle a variety of situations. Regularly review and update the contents to account for changing needs and circumstances.

When it comes to storing your emergency kit, strategic placement is key for accessibility and effectiveness. At home, designate a specific location for your emergency kit and ensure it's readily available for quick access. All family members must be familiar with its location to expedite retrieval in case of an evacuation.

Consider extending your preparedness to your workplace. Have a "grab and go" case stored at work, containing essentials like food, water, medications, and comfortable walking shoes. This ensures you're ready to shelter at work for at least 24 hours if needed. A well-prepared workplace kit can be invaluable during unexpected situations, providing a sense of security and self-sufficiency.

Additionally, your car should serve as an extension of your emergency preparedness. Keep an emergency kit with essential supplies in your car to address potential scenarios where you might be stranded. This kit should include items such as food, water, blankets, and other necessities. Being proactive in preparing for different locations—home, work, and car—bolsters your overall readiness for a variety of emergencies, ensuring you're equipped no matter where you find yourself during a crisis.

Preparedness on a Budget

Firstly, it's crucial to assess the risks and needs specific to your family during potential emergencies. This involves identifying potential challenges in your region, such as natural disasters, social unrest, or power outages, and tailoring your plans accordingly. Prioritize your plan of action based on your family's unique circumstances and vulnerabilities. Consider cost-effective alternatives without compromising on essential elements.

Creating your preparedness strategy involves exploring DIY solutions and maximizing the use of items you already own. Adapt and repurpose existing resources to fulfill multiple roles in your preparedness plan. Additionally, allocate resources wisely by setting a budget that aligns with your financial situation. Prioritize spending on critical items while considering long-term investments. Set realistic financial limits and explore sales, discounts, and bulk purchasing options to maximize savings.

Saving for emergencies is essential. Establish a savings fund dedicated to emergency preparedness, and regularly contribute to ensure ongoing efforts. Seek out smart purchasing opportunities, opting for quality items that offer long-term value and durability. Efficient storage solutions are key, and you can organize and store your emergency supplies using cost-effective methods. Implement a rotation system to ensure stored items remain fresh and usable.

Incorporate community resources into your preparedness efforts by inquiring about available assistance. Collaborate with neighbors, friends, or local community groups for joint preparedness efforts, leveraging shared resources and skills to enhance preparation on a budget. Think ahead by considering future needs and trends, investing in items that serve multiple purposes and that may be useful in evolving situations. Foster adaptability and flexibility in your mindset, adjusting plans based on changing circumstances and available resources.

Regularly review and evaluate your emergency preparedness plans and budget allocations. Identify any gaps or areas that may require additional attention, adjusting plans accordingly. Stay informed about new developments in emergency preparedness, and update plans based on the latest recommendations, technologies, or resources. Reassess your budget periodically to accommodate changes in your financial situation and adjust allocations based on shifting priorities or financial capabilities. Lastly, consider community or skill exchanges to acquire items or services that contribute to preparedness without straining your budget.

As we move forward into the importance of preparedness, let's draw inspiration from Ecclesiastes 7:12: "For wisdom is a defense, and money is a defense: but the excellency of knowledge is, that wisdom giveth life to them that have it" (*King James Bible*, 2023a). This profound verse emphasizes the role of wisdom and knowledge in safeguarding and sustaining life. Our journey toward preparedness highlights the value of acquiring knowledge, making informed decisions, and cultivating the wisdom necessary to navigate the uncertainties that life may present. Let this verse serve as a guiding light, encouraging us to seek knowledge and wisdom as essential defenses in our pursuit of readiness.

SECURING YOUR HOME

A s we dive into the pages ahead, we're on a mission together —to create a haven that's not just safe but fortified with practical security measures and responsible firearm use. And to kick things off, let's draw inspiration from Psalms 127:1: "Except the Lord build the house, they labor in vain that build it: except the Lord keep the city, the watchman waketh but in vain" (*King James Bible*, 2024f).

This verse speaks directly to us, reminding us that building a secure home involves a partnership between our efforts and a higher purpose. Now, let's embark on this journey and explore the critical steps to make our homes resilient and safe, embracing the wisdom from the Psalms as our guiding light.

PRACTICAL HOME SECURITY ADVICE

Ask yourself, what's the easiest way to break into your home?

Understanding the vulnerabilities of your home is foundational to fortifying its security. By conducting a comprehensive security audit, you can gain valuable insights into potential entry points and weak spots that might be exploited by intruders. This proactive approach not only enhances your overall security but also empowers you to take targeted measures to effectively address specific vulnerabilities.

Begin by scrutinizing all possible entry points, including doors, windows, garage doors, and even less obvious areas like basement access points. Look for and identify weak spots such as outdated or rusted locks, flimsy doors, or windows that can easily be broken or forced open.

Evaluate the exterior of your home. Are there areas with inadequate lighting or overgrown vegetation that could provide cover for intruders? Assess the condition of fencing and gates to ensure they are sturdy and well-maintained.

Review the effectiveness of your surveillance and alarm systems. Ensure that cameras cover critical areas and that alarms are strategically placed to provide maximum coverage. Regularly check and test these systems to guarantee they are in working order.

Analyze the overall security of your property's perimeter. Consider whether fencing or natural barriers are sufficient and in good condition. Well-maintained boundaries act as a deterrent and contribute significantly to overall security.

Consider your own patterns of behavior and routines. Understanding when your home is typically occupied or vacant allows you to adjust security measures accordingly. This awareness can influence decisions, such as when to activate alarm systems or increase vigilance.

Based on the audit findings, prioritize necessary upgrades. This might involve installing stronger locks, reinforcing doors and windows, or upgrading to more advanced security systems.

Motion-activated lights can be particularly effective in deterring intruders and eliminating potential hiding spots.

Trim bushes and trees near windows and entrances to eliminate potential hiding spots. An unobstructed view of your property enhances overall security.

Consider joining or forming a neighborhood watch. Collaborative efforts with neighbors can significantly contribute to enhancing overall security in the community.

By taking these steps, you actively address vulnerabilities and create a more resilient and secure home environment. A proactive and vigilant approach to home security is a crucial aspect to ensure the safety and well-being of your household. Let's look at some more safety measures you may want to consider.

1. Keep the doors and windows locked. Seems simple, right? Yet, it's a fundamental practice that is often overlooked. Regularly check and reinforce window and door locks to deter unauthorized access.
2. Install dummy cams. While actual security cameras are effective, dummy cameras can act as a deterrent. Strategically positioning them around your property can create the impression of extensive surveillance.
3. Install alarms. Invest in a reliable alarm system as contemporary systems provide not only intrusion detection but also fire and carbon monoxide alerts, thus enhancing overall safety.
4. Secure your perimeter. Fencing, gates, and well-lit boundaries contribute to a secure perimeter. This not only dissuades potential intruders but also creates a visible boundary.

5. Ensure situational awareness. Encourage a vigilant mindset among your household members. Awareness of surroundings can prevent security lapses.

6. Don't brag about new toys. Be cautious about sharing expensive purchases on social media. Broadcasting new acquisitions can attract unwanted attention.

7. Remember that appearances are everything. Maintain the appearance of an active and cared-for property. A well-kept home suggests occupancy and diligence.

8. Proper exterior lighting, especially near entry points, reduces hiding spots for potential intruders. Motion-activated lights can be particularly effective.

9. Train everyone in your home. Educate all members on security protocols. From locking doors to recognizing suspicious behavior, a united and informed household is a secure one.

Develop a Home Safety Strategy

Developing a home safety strategy is a crucial step in ensuring the well-being of your household during various emergencies. It involves comprehensive planning and preparation for different scenarios, ranging from fire emergencies to potential intrusions. By establishing a well-thought-out strategy, you empower your family members with the knowledge and tools to respond effectively in times of crisis.

Planning for Various Scenarios

A robust home safety strategy encompasses a range of emergency scenarios. This includes defining fire escape routes, outlining communication plans, and preparing for severe weather events. By addressing diverse situations, you ensure that everyone in your household is aware of the appropriate actions to take in different emergencies.

Setting up a Safe Room

Consider designating a safe room within your home—a secure space where family members can retreat during intrusions or severe weather incidents. Equip this room with essentials such as water, non-perishable food, a first aid kit, and communication devices. The safe room serves as a refuge, providing a secure and well-prepared space for your family in critical situations.

Regular Maintenance Checks

The effectiveness of your security systems is contingent upon their operational status. Conduct regular maintenance checks on alarms, surveillance cameras, and locks to ensure they function correctly. Regular inspections and upkeep contribute to the reliability of your security measures, providing consistent protection.

By addressing any issues promptly, you enhance the overall security of your home.

Peace of Mind Through Vigilance

Implementing these practices not only establishes a safer home environment but also contributes to peace of mind. Knowing that your family is well-prepared for emergencies and that your security systems are consistently maintained fosters a sense of security and confidence.

Regular Reassessment

Home safety is an evolving concern, and it's essential to adapt your strategies accordingly. Regularly reassess your security measures to account for changes in family dynamics, technology upgrades, or alterations to your home's layout. This proactive approach ensures that your safety strategies remain effective and up-to-date.

Ensuring the security of your home during natural disasters is paramount to safeguarding your family and possessions. Proper preparation involves understanding the potential threats posed by various natural disasters and taking proactive measures to mitigate risks.

Different regions are susceptible to specific types of natural disasters, such as hurricanes, floods, earthquakes, tornados, or wildfires. Understanding the prevalent risks in your area is the first step to creating an effective home security plan.

Conduct a thorough assessment of your home's vulnerabilities concerning potential disasters. For example, if you live in an earthquake-prone region, focus on securing heavy furniture and appliances to prevent them from toppling. In a flood-prone area, you would keep all essential utilities at higher levels.

Performing a home vulnerability assessment involves evaluating the structural integrity of your residence. Identify weak points in the building, such as outdated roofing, cracks in walls, or inadequate foundation support. Addressing these vulnerabilities can enhance the overall resilience of your home. Plus, by doing all these security upgrades, you also increase the value of your home, so it's a win in every way.

Engage in a systematic evaluation of your property's susceptibility to natural disasters. This involves inspecting the exterior and interior of your home, checking for potential hazards, and ensuring that safety measures are in place. Common weak points include doors and windows that may not withstand high winds, unstable roofing, and unsecured outdoor structures. Reinforce doors and windows with impact-resistant materials, secure loose roof shingles, and fortify structures like sheds and fences.

Create a plan to secure valuable items and essential documents. Invest in a waterproof and fireproof safe to store important documents, passports, and valuable possessions. Consider digital backups for critical data. Tailor your home security measures to the specific risks associated with the prevalent natural disasters in your area. Install storm shutters for hurricane protection, elevate electrical systems for flood prevention, and reinforce foundations for earthquake resistance.

By understanding the potential threats, conducting thorough assessments, and implementing targeted measures, you significantly enhance your home's resilience against natural disasters. Proactive planning and mitigation strategies contribute to the safety and well-being of your family and the preservation of your property during challenging times.

FIREARMS AND SAFE USAGE

Owning a firearm for home protection is a great investment, but it does come with responsibilities. It's crucial to prioritize safe storage and handling, recognizing that proper firearm management is integral to ensuring the safety of everyone in your household.

Investing in a high-quality gun safe or lockbox equipped with secure locking mechanisms offers a physical barrier, effectively preventing unauthorized access to firearms. Look for safes with robust locking systems, such as combination locks or biometric features, to add an extra layer of security.

Store firearms and ammunition separately to reduce the risk of accidental discharge. Use dedicated containers or safes for ammunition, ensuring they are kept in a secure location away from firearms. Choose a storage location that is only accessible to responsible adults in your household.

Educate all family members, especially children, on firearm safety. Establish clear guidelines that guns are not toys and should never be handled without proper supervision. Teach children the basic principles of firearm safety, such as always treating a gun as if it's loaded and never pointing it at anyone. Creating awareness within the family fosters a culture of safety and responsible behavior. Remember, safe storage is not just about physical barriers but also about instilling a sense of responsibility and awareness within your household.

Treat every firearm as if it is loaded, regardless of your belief in its status. This mindset instills a habit of careful handling, minimizing the risk of accidents. Always verify the condition of the firearm before any interaction.

Maintain a strict discipline of always pointing the muzzle in a safe direction. Whether handling or storing a firearm, ensure that the muzzle is directed away from people and objects you do not intend to shoot.

Should the need arise for you to use a firearm, remember to place your finger on the trigger only when you're prepared to fire. Before taking any shot, be fully aware of your target and what lies beyond it. Ensure a clear and safe firing range to prevent unintended consequences.

When transporting firearms, ensure all firearms are unloaded and securely stored during transit. Adhering to transportation laws is crucial to prevent accidents and unauthorized access whether traveling to the range or relocating firearms.

In the unfortunate event of a lost or stolen firearm, promptly report it to law enforcement. Reporting ensures that the authorities can take necessary actions to recover the firearm and prevent its potential misuse.

Maintaining proficiency with your firearm is key. Engage in regular training sessions to practice proper aiming, reloading, and addressing malfunctions in a controlled environment. This ongoing training enhances your familiarity with the firearm and builds your confidence and muscle memory ensuring you can handle it safely and effectively should you ever need to defend your family.

Enroll in a reputable firearm safety course, these courses provide essential knowledge about safe gun handling, proper storage practices, and the responsible use of firearms. Participating in such courses equips gun owners with the skills and understanding needed to maintain a safe environment.

Of course, let's not forget about the legal aspects. Laws regarding firearm usage vary by location, and gun owners must comply with local, state, and federal regulations. A comprehensive understanding of these laws prevents legal issues. Stay informed about updates in firearm safety practices and legislation. Ongoing education ensures that you remain up-to-date on any changes in laws or recommended safety procedures.

Responsible gun ownership is a multifaceted commitment that encompasses safe storage at home and conscientious practices during transportation. By integrating these responsible habits into daily firearm management, gun owners actively contribute to a culture of safety, compliance, and community well-being.

ADAPTING SECURITY TO LIVING SITUATIONS

Security measures should be as unique as the place you call home. Recognizing the distinct characteristics of your living situation is crucial for an effective and personalized security approach.

In a world where diversity extends to living arrangements, the cookie-cutter approach to security falls short. What works for a suburban house might not be suitable for an urban apartment or a mobile home. And the needs of a rural homestead greatly differ from those of a mobile home. Embracing this diversity requires a tailored strategy that considers the specific challenges and opportunities presented by each living situation.

Apartments

Living in an apartment offers comfort and convenience, but it also brings unique security considerations. Whether you're a renter or someone with limited modification permissions, fortifying security in an apartment demands strategic and creative solutions.

Reinforcing Door Frames

Door frames are often the first line of defense. Strengthening them with security plates or reinforcements makes it harder for intruders to force their way in. For renters, non-permanent solutions like door frame reinforcement kits are effective without violating lease agreements.

Doorstop Alarms

Simple yet effective, doorstop alarms serve as an audible deterrent. Placed under doors, they emit a loud sound if someone attempts to force the door open. This not only alerts the residents but also alerts neighbors, enhancing the overall security of the building.

Apartment-Compatible Security Systems

Investing in a security system designed for apartment living is a smart move. These systems are often wireless, allowing easy installation without drilling holes or running extensive cables. Look for features like motion sensors, door/window alarms, and smartphone compatibility for convenient monitoring.

Collaborative Security

Apartments offer a unique advantage—proximity to neighbors. Establishing a collaborative security effort with neighbors enhances the overall safety of the building. Encourage open communication about any suspicious activities, and consider forming a neighborhood watch group. Collective vigilance can deter potential threats and create a sense of community security.

Respecting Rental Constraints

For renters, it's crucial to respect lease agreements and limitations on modifications. Fortunately, many security measures exist that don't breach these constraints. Portable door barricades, security cameras that don't require drilling, and smart doorbell cameras are viable options that offer enhanced security without jeopardizing your lease.

When living in an apartment, security is a shared responsibility. Strategic choices and collaboration with neighbors can significantly improve the safety of the entire building. By adopting apartment-compatible security solutions and respecting rental constraints, residents can enjoy peace of mind in their urban sanctuaries.

Mobile Homes

Mobile homes offer mobility but require specific security adjustments. Strengthen doors with deadbolts, install window security film, and anchor the home properly. Lightweight and portable security systems tailored to mobile homes provide an extra layer of defense. Being aware of your surroundings and neighbors fosters a collaborative security approach.

Door Security

Strengthen doors with deadbolt locks to fortify entry points. Mobile home doors are typically lighter, making them potential vulnerabilities. Reinforcing them with deadbolts adds an extra layer of protection.

Window Security Film

Install window security film on windows to reinforce them against break-ins. This transparent layer adds durability, making it more difficult for intruders to shatter windows. Opt for security films designed to resist impact and provide an additional barrier.

Proper Anchoring

Mobile homes are susceptible to movement during severe weather or attempted break-ins. Ensure your home is properly anchored to its foundations as this not only enhances security but also prevents structural damage during storms.

Portable Security Systems

Explore lightweight and portable security systems designed specifically for mobile homes. These systems may include wireless alarms, motion sensors, and camera solutions. Their adaptability to the mobile lifestyle provides an extra layer of defense without compromising convenience.

Community Awareness

Stay aware of your surroundings and build rapport with your neighbors in mobile home communities. A collaborative security approach fosters a sense of community vigilance. Share information about any unusual activities, and support each other to maintain a safe living environment.

Emergency Preparedness

Given the mobile nature of these homes, have a well-thought-out emergency plan. Know evacuation routes, emergency contacts, and the location of nearby shelters. Being prepared for both security threats and natural disasters is essential in a mobile home setting.

Fire Safety

Mobile homes may have unique fire safety considerations. Install smoke detectors and fire extinguishers, and regularly check their functionality. Educate all occupants about fire escape routes and conduct fire drills regularly.

Securing a mobile home involves a combination of structural reinforcement, technological solutions, and community awareness. By addressing these aspects, residents can enjoy their homes while ensuring a safe and protected living environment.

Rural Homes

In more secluded settings, rural homes face distinct challenges. Invest in outdoor lighting, secure perimeters with fencing, and employ motion-activated cameras. Establishing a close-knit community network enhances vigilance. Additionally, consider a backup power source to ensure that security systems remain operational during outages.

Outdoor Lighting

Rural areas often lack the ambient light of urban settings. Invest in outdoor lighting to eliminate hiding spots and deter potential intruders. Motion-activated lights around entry points, pathways, and outbuildings provide both security and visibility.

Perimeter Security

Securing the perimeter is critical in rural settings. Fencing, especially with features like sturdy gates and strategically placed thorny plants, acts as a deterrent. Regularly inspect and maintain fences to ensure their integrity.

Motion-Activated Cameras

Motion-activated cameras serve as proactive surveillance tools. Install them at key points around your property, such as entrances, driveways, and outbuildings. These cameras not only capture potential threats but also act as a deterrent, signaling that the property is under surveillance.

Community Network

Rural living often fosters close-knit communities, so establishing a network with neighbors promotes mutual vigilance. Share information about any suspicious activities, and collaborate on security initiatives. Rural neighborhoods can benefit significantly from a collective approach to safety.

Backup Power Source

Ensure your security systems remain operational during the event of a power outage by having a backup power source. Generators or solar-powered systems can keep cameras, alarms, and communication systems functioning seamlessly.

Emergency Communication Plan

Create an emergency communication plan with neighbors. In rural areas, where distances between homes can be significant, having a reliable means of communication during emergencies is crucial. This plan should include contact information, meeting points, and procedures to alert others of potential threats.

Firearms Safety

In rural settings where response times may be longer, some residents choose to own firearms for protection. If you decide to do so, prioritize safety as we discussed in the previous section. It's also important to find out from your county sheriff's department what the local and state laws are regarding defending your family and property.

Securing a rural home involves a combination of proactive measures, community collaboration, and adapting to the unique challenges of secluded living. By addressing these considerations, residents can create a safe and resilient environment in their rural retreats.

As Sun Tzu wisely noted, "The greatest victory is that which requires no battle" ("A Quote From *The Art of War*," n.d). This philosophy mirrors the essence of proactive security. By adapting measures to your living situation, you create a fortress that deters conflicts and emergencies, embodying the true victory of preparedness and security.

PREPARING FOR NATURAL DISASTERS

> *Adapt or perish, now as ever, is nature's inexorable imperative.*

— H.G. WELLS

H.G. Wells's profound words echo the timeless truth that adaptation is the key to survival. As we delve into preparing for natural disasters, this quote serves as a guiding light, emphasizing the importance of being adaptable and well-prepared. Nature's unpredictability necessitates our readiness to face and overcome its challenges.

STRATEGIES FOR DIFFERENT NATURAL DISASTERS

When it comes to facing the diverse challenges posed by natural disasters, a well-thought-out strategy can make all the difference. Let's have a look at different natural disasters and what you can do to prepare. This will also involve what you can do during the disaster and how to bounce back afterward.

Floods

Living in flood-prone areas necessitates a proactive approach to ensuring your safety and minimizing damage.

1. Risk Awareness

    A. Research and understand your area's flood risk and elevation levels.
    B. Stay informed about seasonal weather patterns and potential flood triggers.

2. Emergency Kit Readiness

    A. Develop a comprehensive emergency kit that includes non-perishable food, water, and first aid supplies.
    B. Make sure your emergency kit is up-to-date and easily accessible.

3. Elevation Strategies

    A. Identify potential flood levels in your home.
    B. Elevate electrical appliances and utilities above these levels to reduce damage.

During the Flood: Swift and Informed Action

When faced with an imminent flood, taking immediate and informed actions can make a significant difference.

1. Evacuation Readiness

    A. Be prepared to evacuate to higher ground if authorities issue warnings or if you observe signs of flooding.
    B. Plan the safest evacuation routes and destinations.

2. Avoid Hazardous Areas

    A. Steer clear of flooded roads and pathways as water depth can be deceiving, and currents may be strong.
    B. Do not attempt to drive or walk through flooded areas.

3. Information and Communication

    A. Stay tuned to weather updates through reliable sources.
    B. Heed emergency notifications and instructions from local authorities.

Post-Flood: Recovery and Restoration

After the floodwaters recede, the recovery process begins. Ensure a systematic approach for a safe return and effective recovery.

1. Safety First

    A. Return home only when authorities declare it safe to do so.
    B. Exercise caution and be mindful of potential hazards.

2. Home Inspection

    A. Thoroughly inspect your home for damage before entering.
    B. Document any damage with photographs and notes.

3. Insurance Protocol

    A. Contact your insurance company promptly to initiate the claims process.
    B. Provide detailed information about the extent of damage and loss.

By meticulously adhering to these guidelines, you are not only fortifying your resilience against floods but also contributing to a more rapid and efficient recovery process. Remember, preparation is the key to mitigating the impact of natural disasters.

Hurricanes

Being prepared for hurricanes involves a combination of planning, securing your home, and ensuring you have essential supplies.

1. Evacuation Readiness

    A. Make sure to familiarize yourself and everyone in your family with designated evacuation routes.
    B. It's important to have an emergency plan in place, which should include communication strategies and designated meeting points.

2. Home Fortification

    A. Secure windows and doors using storm shutters or plywood.
    B. Reinforce garage doors to minimize vulnerability during high winds.

3. Essential Supplies Stockpiling

    A. Create an emergency kit with non-perishable food, an ample water supply, and essential medications.
    B. Ensure you have sufficient supplies to sustain your family for several days.

During the Hurricane: Safe Shelter and Preparedness

When a hurricane is imminent, taking shelter and staying informed are crucial elements of your safety plan.

1. Indoor Safety

    A. Stay indoors and away from windows and glass doors throughout the hurricane.
    B. Seek refuge in a designated safe room, preferably in the center of your home.

2. Information Access

    A. Utilize a battery-powered weather radio to stay updated on the hurricane's progress.
    B. Follow official announcements and weather advisories for real-time information.

3. Power Outage Preparedness

A. Anticipate power outages, and equip yourself with alternative lighting sources such as flashlights and lanterns.
B. Keep a sufficient supply of batteries and charging solutions for electronic devices.

Post-Hurricane: Returning and Recovery

Once the hurricane has passed, a methodical approach to assessing damage and initiating recovery is essential.

1. Safety Verification

A. Wait for authorities to declare it safe before returning home.
B. Exercise caution when reentering your property, and be aware of potential dangers.

2. Property Inspection

A. Check for structural damage, including the roof, walls, and foundation problems.
B. Address immediate hazards and secure the premises.

3. Insurance Protocols

A. Remember to contact your insurance company as soon as possible to report damages.
B. Document damage thoroughly with photographs and detailed descriptions for insurance claims.

Earthquakes

Being prepared for earthquakes and implementing safety measures not only enhances your ability to respond effectively but also ensures the safety of those you love.

1. Securing Home Contents

   A. Fasten heavy furniture and appliances to walls to prevent them from toppling during seismic activity.
   B. Install latches on cabinets to secure items inside.

2. Emergency Kit Essentials

   A. Assemble a well-stocked emergency kit that contains essential supplies.
   B. Make sure to include sturdy closed-toe shoes, a flash-light, and a battery-powered radio in your kit.

3. Drop, Cover, and Hold on

   A. Familiarize yourself with the "drop, cover, and hold on" technique. These are the recommended actions to exercise during an earthquake.
   B. Practice this technique during family drills to ensure everyone knows how to respond swiftly.

During the Earthquake: Immediate Actions for Safety

1. Drop, Cover, and Hold on

   A. Drop to the ground to prevent being knocked over.
   B. Take cover under a sturdy piece of furniture to shield yourself from falling objects.
   C. Hold on until the shaking subsides to ensure your safety.

2. Indoor Safety Measures

   A. Stay indoors during the earthquake, away from windows, heavy furniture, and appliances.
   B. Seek refuge in a safe area, such as under a sturdy table or against an interior wall.

3. Outdoor Safety Guidelines

   A. If outside, move to an open area away from buildings, trees, and streetlights.
   B. Avoid structures, signs, and utility wires that could pose a hazard.

Post-Earthquake: Assessing and Responding

1. Injury Evaluation and First Aid

   A. Check for injuries among family members, and administer first aid as needed.
   B. Prioritize medical attention for severe injuries, and promptly seek professional help.

2. Hazard Inspection

A. Inspect your surroundings for potential hazards, such as structural damage or gas leaks.
B. Address immediate dangers, such as unstable structures or fallen debris.

3. Aftershock Preparedness

A. Be mentally prepared for aftershocks, which may follow the initial earthquake.
B. Reinforce safety measures and remain cautious in the aftermath.

Tornados

1. Safe Room Identification

A. Identify a safe room in your home, preferably in the basement or an interior room on the lowest floor.
B. Reinforce this space with sturdy construction to provide maximum protection.

2. Weather Radio Essential

A. Equip yourself with an NOAA Weather Radio to receive timely tornado warnings.
B. Familiarize yourself with the emergency alerts and warnings system for your region.

3. Securing Outdoor Items

   A. Secure outdoor items that could become projectiles during high winds.
   B. Store or anchor loose objects to prevent them from causing damage or injury.

During the Tornado: Immediate Actions for Survival

1. Basement or Interior Room Shelter

   A. During severe weather, seek shelter in a basement or an interior room on the lowest floor of your home.
   B. Choose a space away from windows, preferably in the center of your home.

2. Protective Measures

   A. Avoid windows, and cover yourself with a mattress, heavy blankets, or any available sturdy furniture.
   B. Consider using additional protective gear, such as helmets, to minimize the risk of head injuries.

3. Outdoor Shelter Procedures

   A. If caught outside, find a low-lying area like a ditch or depression.
   B. Lie flat and cover your head to minimize exposure to flying debris.

Post-Tornado: Navigating the Aftermath Safely

1. Waiting for Clearance

   A. Wait for authorities to declare it safe before leaving your shelter.
   B. Remain vigilant and attentive to ongoing weather updates.

2. Hazards Assessment

   A. Watch for hazards like downed power lines, broken glass, and debris.
   B. Exercise caution while navigating the affected area, avoiding potential dangers.

3. Community Assistance

   A. Check on neighbors and offer assistance if needed.
   B. Collaborate with local community resources to ensure the well-being of everyone affected.

Wildfires

1. Defensible Space Establishment

   A. Create a defensible space around your home by clearing brush, dead vegetation, and debris.
   B. Maintain a buffer zone to impede the rapid spread of wildfires toward your property.

2. Emergency Kit and Evacuation Plan

A. Assemble an emergency kit with essentials like food, water, important documents, and first aid supplies.
B. Develop a thorough evacuation plan, ensuring all family members understand and practice it.

3. Monitoring Authorities and Weather

A. Stay informed by monitoring local authorities' alerts and weather updates.
B. Be prepared to act swiftly based on official recommendations and evolving wildfire conditions.

During the Wildfire: Immediate Actions for Personal Safety

1. Evacuation Preparedness

A. Evacuate promptly if authorities recommend or if you feel threatened by the approaching wildfire.
B. Prioritize personal safety, and adhere to evacuation routes provided by emergency services.

2. Indoor Safety Measures

A. Stay indoors if evacuation is not possible, keeping windows and doors closed to prevent smoke infiltration.
B. Utilize N95 masks to filter smoke particles if air quality becomes compromised.

Post-Wildfire: Returning Home Safely and Assessing Damage

1. Waiting for Clearance

    A. Wait for authorities to declare it safe before returning home.
    B. Avoid entering the area until you have been given the green light to ensure continued safety.

2. Property Inspection

    A. Inspect your property for embers, smoldering materials, and potential fire hazards.
    B. Address any lingering threats to prevent reignition or further damage.

3. Cautious Exploration

    A. Exercise caution in areas affected by the wildfire, considering unstable terrain and potential ash pits.
    B. Follow safety guidelines during cleanup and restoration efforts.

By using these strategies to prepare for different natural disasters, you fortify your home against threats and enhance your ability to navigate these challenging natural events with resilience and preparedness.

CREATING A FAMILY EMERGENCY PLAN

When it comes to safeguarding your family in times of crisis, having a comprehensive emergency plan is paramount. Gather your family for an open discussion about potential hazards and emergencies, and encourage everyone to share their concerns and insights.

Begin by mapping local routes leading out of your neighborhood, marking both primary and alternative options. Consider various transportation modes, such as cars, bicycles, or walking, and plan routes suitable for each mode, ensuring flexibility in evacuation methods. Identify community resources like shelters, emergency assistance centers, or safe zones, and collaborate with neighbors to share information about communal evacuation strategies. Consider heading to family or friends outside the affected area for safety and support.

Start talking to your extended family and friends who live in safer zones. Work out a joint evacuation plan, covering everything from routes to meeting points. This collaborative effort ensures everyone is on the same page and ready to support each other. Teaming up with family and friends not only makes practical sense but also builds a shared strength. Knowing you have a place to go during tough times not only eases the logistical burden but also provides emotional support that can make all the difference. Familiar surroundings and the support of family and friends help reduce the impact of the disaster, especially on children, making the situation more manageable.

When designating evacuation destinations, choose local options like community centers or schools as primary points, and establish alternatives based on the nature of the emergency. Consider out-of-area contacts as rallying points, providing flexibility if local options are compromised. Share the evacuation plan with all family members, ensuring everyone understands the routes, meeting points, and contact information.

Establish a list of emergency contacts, including local authorities, family, and friends, to ensure you have support readily available during times of need. Share this list with all family members and keep a copy in your emergency kit. Identify primary and secondary communication channels, including text messages, calls, and social media, ensuring everyone has access to these channels and understands their use. Include a battery-powered or hand-crank emergency radio in your kit to receive updates and instructions, and familiarize family members with its operation.

Assigning roles and responsibilities is a key aspect of the communication plan. Designate a communication coordinator responsible for coordinating communications and ensuring that messages are relayed and received effectively. Assign specific roles to family members based on their capabilities and strengths, such as gathering essential documents, securing pets, or assisting vulnerable family members. Establish regular check-in times during emergencies, ensuring each family member reports their status, location, and any emerging needs.

Practice Your Plan

Regularly conduct practice drills for your evacuation plan. Include various scenarios such as fires, earthquakes, or severe weather to test the readiness of your family members. Drills enhance familiarity with procedures and boost confidence in executing the plan. These drills can be a fun family activity, like building shelters or assembling kits. This is a great way to spend time together and teach your children what they need to do in the type of emergency you are preparing for.

After each drill, conduct a thorough review session to identify areas for improvement. Adjust the plan based on the lessons learned during practice. This process ensures that your emergency plan remains effective and responsive to evolving circumstances.

Creating a family emergency plan is an ongoing process that demands regular attention. It is crucial to revisit and update the plan to address changes in family dynamics, living situations, or community resources. A well-thought-out and regularly practiced plan empowers your family to face uncertainties with resilience and coordinated efficiency.

When I think of everything I need to do to be prepared and provide safety for my family, this scripture, Isaiah 43:2, often comes to mind: "When thou passest through the waters, I will be with thee; and through the rivers, they shall not overflow thee: when thou walkest through the fire, thou shalt not be burned; neither shall the flame kindle upon thee" (*King James Bible*, 2015).

For me, it serves as a beacon of hope and resilience, assuring us that even in the face of life's trials, there is divine protection. As you fortify your family with an emergency plan, let the spirit of resilience that is inspired by these words guide your preparations, instilling confidence to face any challenge that may arise.

LONG-TERM FOOD AND WATER STORAGE

Throughout the journey of preparedness, ensuring a sustainable supply of food and water takes center stage. This chapter delves into the vital techniques and considerations that empower you to manage sustenance needs over extended periods. Embarking on the path of long-term preparedness echoes the wisdom found in Genesis 41:36: "And that food shall be for store to the land against the seven years of famine" (*King James Bible*, 2024a). This verse encapsulates the essence of foresight and preparation—a timeless lesson applicable to our situations.

TECHNIQUES FOR LONG-TERM FOOD STORAGE: PRESERVING THE BOUNTY

Understanding the factors that contribute to food spoilage is the foundation for effective preservation. Let's explore these elements and how they impact the longevity of stored food.

1. Microorganisms

Microorganisms, such as bacteria, yeast, and mold, are silent culprits that hasten food spoilage. They thrive in moisture-rich environments, breaking down nutrients and causing decay. Properly sealing and removing moisture through techniques like dehydration or canning are effective defenses against microbial invasion.

2. Enzymes

Enzymes are natural components in food that, when activated, promote ripening and decay. Blanching or cooking food before storage deactivates these enzymes, slowing the deterioration process. Understanding which foods benefit from specific prepa-ration methods is key to enzyme control.

3. Oxygen

Oxygen is a friend to some foods but an enemy to others. It facili-tates the oxidation process, leading to rancidity and nutrient loss. Oxygen absorbers and vacuum-sealing can be used in storage containers to create an oxygen-free environment, significantly extending the shelf life of many food items.

4. Pests

Unwanted guests like insects and rodents can swiftly turn a well-stocked pantry into a feast for them. Make use of practices like sealing food in airtight containers and regularly inspecting storage areas. You might also consider using natural repellents like bay leaves or diatomaceous earth to deter pests.

5. Light

Exposure to light, especially sunlight, can degrade the quality of stored food. It can lead to nutrient loss, discoloration, and flavor changes. Storing food in opaque or dark containers and keeping them in a cool, dark place helps mitigate the degrading effects of light.

Understanding these factors and implementing appropriate measures ensures that your long-term food storage remains a reservoir of nutrition and sustenance. Now, let's look at different preservation techniques and how to use them.

Heat Preservation Methods

Canning

Canning is a traditional method of preserving food by sealing it in airtight containers, typically jars, to prevent spoilage. The process involves heating the food to destroy harmful microorganisms, enzymes, and molds that can cause deterioration. By creating a vacuum seal, canning inhibits the growth of bacteria and other spoilage agents, allowing the food to remain safe and edible for an extended period. There are two canning methods: water bath and pressure canning.

Water bath canning is suitable for preserving high-acid foods like fruits, tomatoes, pickles, and jams. This method involves submerging sealed jars in boiling water for a specific duration to create a vacuum seal. On the contrary, pressure canning is recommended for low-acid foods such as vegetables, meats, poultry, and seafood. However, it requires a specialized pressure canner to reach temperatures beyond boiling, ensuring the safety of the preserved food.

Use only fresh, high-quality produce for the best results, and follow tested and approved canning recipes to ensure safety. Properly sterilize jars, lids, and utensils to prevent contamination, and adhere to recommended processing times and methods based on the type of food and canning technique. You can check out the following sources for a more in-depth guide on home canning:

- National Center for Home Food Preservation | USDA Publications (uga.edu)
- How to Can: A Beginner's Guide to Canning Food (ballmasonjars.com)

Canning Steps:

1. Selecting Fresh Produce

    A. Choose fruits or vegetables at their peak freshness.
    B. Opt for high-quality produce without blemishes or signs of decay.

2. Sterilizing Jars and Lids

    A. Wash jars, lids, and bands in hot, soapy water.
    B. Sterilize them by boiling jars and lids for 10 minutes.
    C. Keep jars warm until they are ready to be filled.

3. Packing Food Into Jars

    A. Pack prepared produce into sterilized jars, leaving recommended headspace.
    B. Use a non-metallic utensil to remove air bubbles and ensure even packing.

4. Adding Canning Liquid

    A. Choose a suitable canning liquid—water, syrup, or brine —based on the type of food being canned.
    B. Ensure the liquid covers the produce while maintaining the specified headspace.

5. Processing in a Water Bath or Pressure Canner

    A. Follow recommended processing times and pressures for the specific food and canning method.
    B. Water bath canning is suitable for high-acid foods, while

pressure canning is ideal for low-acid foods.

Dehydration

Dehydration is a time-honored food preservation technique that involves removing moisture from food, slowing down the growth of spoilage microorganisms and bacteria. By eliminating water content, dehydration inhibits the enzymatic reactions responsible for spoilage, effectively extending the shelf life of various foods. This method not only preserves the nutritional value of the food but also results in lightweight, space-efficient storage.

Dehydration Steps:

1. Slice or Chop Food

    A. Slice or chop food into uniform pieces for consistent drying.
    B. Ensure pieces are of similar thickness to promote even dehydration.

2. Arrange Dehydrator Trays

    A. Lay prepared food pieces on dehydrator trays, allowing space for air circulation.
    B. Avoid overcrowding to ensure efficient drying.

3. Set Dehydrator Temperature

    A. Refer to specific temperature guidelines for different foods, which can be found in the user guide.
    B. Generally, temperatures range between 125°F and 160°F (52°C and 71°C).

4. Dry to the Desired Moisture Content

    A. Monitor the drying process, checking for pliability and lack of moisture.
    B. Achieve the desired moisture content for optimal storage.

5. Store in Airtight Containers

    A. Use airtight containers to store dehydrated food.
    B. Consider adding oxygen absorbers to extend shelf life.

Pasteurization

Pasteurization is a heat treatment process applied to liquids, primarily aimed at enhancing their safety by reducing or eliminating harmful microorganisms, such as bacteria, viruses, and yeasts. This technique plays a crucial role in preventing spoilage, extending shelf life, and ensuring that liquids remain safe for consumption. There are three different pasteurization techniques:

Low-Temperature/Long-Time (LTLT):

- The liquid is heated to approximately 145°F (63°C) for at least 30 minutes.
- This is commonly used for dairy products such as milk.

High-Temperature/Short-Time (HTST):

- The liquid is heated to around 161°F (72°C) for about 15 seconds.
- This is widely used for various beverages, including fruit juices.

Ultra-Pasteurization:

- Liquid is subjected to even higher temperatures, typically between 280°F and 302°F (138°C and 150°C), for a shorter time.
- This extends shelf life further and is commonly employed for dairy and plant-based milk alternatives.

Pasteurization Steps:

1. Heat to the Specific Temperature

A. Heat liquids to a specific temperature, typically between 145°F and 160°F (63°C and 71°C).
B. Maintain this temperature for a set duration based on the type of liquid.

2. Cool Quickly

    A. Cool pasteurized liquids rapidly to prevent overcooking.
    B. Use an ice bath or other efficient cooling method.

3. Store in Sterilized Containers

    A. Pour pasteurized liquid into sterilized containers, leaving appropriate headspace.
    B. Seal containers tightly to prevent contamination.

Evaporation

Evaporation is a preservation method that involves the removal of water from liquids, concentrating their flavors, and preserving their shelf life. This process, widely used in the food and beverage industry, helps create concentrated solutions, extracts, or syrups. By reducing the water content, evaporation inhibits the growth of microorganisms, preventing spoilage and extending the longevity of liquids.

1. Heat Liquids

    A. Apply heat to liquids to promote water evaporation.
    B. Use a gentle heat source to avoid scorching.

2. Condense Vapors

    A. Capture evaporated vapors and condense them into a concentrated liquid.
    B. Utilize a condenser or cooling system for this process.

3. Store Concentrated Liquid

A. Store the condensed liquid in sterilized containers.
B. Ensure airtight seals to prevent rehydration.

Sun Drying

Sun drying, also referred to as solar drying, is a traditional method of preserving food that harnesses the energy of the sun to remove moisture from food items. This ancient technique has been utilized across various cultures to preserve fruits, vegetables, herbs, and meats. The process entails exposing food to direct sunlight and airflow, facilitating the gradual evaporation of water content while inhibiting the growth of microorganisms.

1. Prepare Fruits and Vegetables

A. Slice or halve fruits and vegetables into uniform pieces.
B. Choose items with high water content for optimal results.

2. Arrange on Drying Racks

A. Place prepared items on drying racks.
B. Ensure racks are elevated to allow air circulation.

3. Turn Regularly

A. Rotate and turn items regularly to ensure even drying.
B. Protect from insects and debris during the process.

4. Store in a Cool, Dark Place

A. After sun-drying, store items in a cool, dark place.
B. Consider vacuum-sealed bags for prolonged freshness.

Smoking

Smoking involves exposing food, typically meat and fish, to smoke produced by burning or smoldering wood chips or other flavor-enhancing materials. There are different types, shapes, and sizes of smokers which you should be able to buy at an outdoor retailer or online. Beyond preservation, smoking imparts a distinctive flavor and color to the food, enhancing its taste and visual appeal. This technique has been employed for centuries across various cultures to extend the shelf life of perishable foods and create unique, smoky flavors.

1. Cure With Salt Mixture

A. Apply a salt mixture to the meat for curing.
B. Allow the mixture to penetrate for flavor and preservation.

2. Cold-Smoke With Hardwood Chips

A. Cold-smoke meat using hardwood chips for a prolonged period.
B. Control temperature to impart flavor without cooking.

3. Ensure Ideal Preservation

A. Monitor the smoking process to achieve desired preservation.

B. Store smoked meat in a cool, dry environment.

Cold Preservation Methods

Cold preservation is an important step to extend shelf life and maintain the freshness of perishable items to prevent spoilage.

Refrigeration

Refrigeration is a cornerstone of modern food preservation, offering a controlled environment to slow down bacterial growth and enzymatic reactions.

1. Temperature Control

- Set your refrigerator at or below 40°F (4°C) to effectively inhibit bacterial proliferation.

Airtight Storage

- Keep perishable items in airtight containers or wrap them tightly to prevent the absorption of odors and maintain optimal freshness.

Freezing

Freezing is a potent method to halt microbial activity, preserving food for an extended period.

1. Proper Packaging

- To prevent freezer burn and maintain the quality of food, package it in airtight, freezer-safe containers or vacuum-sealed bags.

2. Labeling

- Clearly label containers with the date and contents to facilitate organized rotation and prevent food waste.

3. Temperature Maintenance

- Ensure your freezer operates at a temperature of 0°F (-18°C) or lower for safe and effective preservation.

Root Cellar

Root cellars hark back to traditional methods of cold storage, especially for root vegetables. These subterranean spaces offer a cool, dark, and humid environment ideal for preserving produce.

1. Bury Vegetables

- Store vegetables like potatoes, carrots, and onions underground to capitalize on the cool, dark conditions.

2. Regular Inspection

- Periodically check for signs of spoilage, promptly removing any affected items to prevent the spread of deterioration.

Chemical Methods

Chemical preservation methods involve the use of natural compounds like vinegar, salt, and sugar to not only extend shelf life but also enhance flavors.

Vinegar Pickling

Vinegar pickling is a centuries-old method that imparts a tangy and flavorful twist to vegetables or fruits.

1. Submerge in a Vinegar Solution

- Immerse vegetables or fruits in a vinegar solution, creating an acidic environment that inhibits bacterial growth.

2. Herbs and Spices Infusion

- Add desired herbs and spices to enhance flavor complexity.

3. Store

- Store the pickled produce in sterilized jars to maintain a clean and safe environment.

Lactic Acid Fermentation

This method harnesses the power of natural fermentation to both preserve and cultivate unique flavors.

1. Submerge in Saltwater Brine

- Submerge vegetables in a brine solution, usually consisting of salt and water, creating an environment conducive to fermentation.

2. Natural Fermentation

- Allow the natural fermentation process to occur, producing lactic acid, which acts as a preservative.

This method is particularly suited for preserving vegetables, like cucumbers as pickles or cabbage as sauerkraut. For more information, you can visit the National Library of Medicine: Lactic Acid Fermentations - Applications of Biotechnology to Fermented Foods - NCBI Bookshelf (Steinkraus, 2024).

Salt Curing

Salt curing is a time-honored technique primarily used to preserve meats.

1. Salt Mixture Coverage

- Cover meat with a mixture of salt and, at times, sugar or herbs, forming a preserving layer.

2. Moisture Extraction

- Allow the salt to draw out moisture from the meat, creating an inhospitable environment for bacteria.

3. Rinse and Air-Dry

- Rinse the cured meat to remove excess salt and air-dry it before storing.

Sugar Curing

Sugar curing is a sweet preservation method, ideal for fruits.

1. Sugarcoat

   • Coat fruit in sugar to draw out moisture, creating a syrupy solution.

2. Syrup Creation

   • Use the released fruit juices to create a syrup that further aids preservation.

This method is particularly suitable for preserving delicate fruits like berries.

Customize your long-term food storage strategy based on your preferences and the nature of the food items you wish to preserve.

Choosing the Right Storage Containers: Safeguarding Your Long-Term Supplies

When storing food for the long term, choosing the right containers is essential to preserve freshness and prevent spoilage. Here's an overview of various storage containers and their suitability.

Glass Jars

Glass jars are a timeless option for preserving and storing foods. Their transparency allows for easy visibility, and they are inert, meaning they won't react with the stored contents. To use glass jars for long-term storage, ensure they have a dependable airtight seal to prevent the entry of moisture and air. Additionally, store the jars in a cool, dark place to avoid exposure to light, which can degrade certain foods over time.

PETE Containers

Polyethylene terephthalate (PETE) containers are commonly used for food and beverage packaging as they're lightweight, durable, and resistant to moisture and chemicals. To use PETE containers for long-term storage, look for the recycling code "1" on the bottom of the container, indicating it's made of PETE. Clean containers thoroughly and ensure they are dry before filling them with food. Also, avoid storing PETE containers in high-temperature environments.

Mylar Bags

These popular bags are an excellent option for storing dehydrated or freeze-dried foods because they provide a barrier against light, moisture, and oxygen. To enhance their effectiveness, you can include oxygen absorbers to create an oxygen-free environment. This helps extend food longevity by ensuring a secure and airtight seal, preventing air and moisture from entering the bags.

Oxygen Absorbers

Oxygen absorbers are small packets that typically contain iron powder, salt, and clay. They function by absorbing oxygen from the air, thus preventing oxidation and extending the shelf life of stored food. To utilize oxygen absorbers effectively, include them in containers before sealing to maintain a low-oxygen environment. It's crucial to use the right-sized absorbers for the volume of the container to ensure effectiveness in preserving the food.

Buckets

Food-grade plastic buckets with airtight lids are ideal for storing bulk items. It's important to ensure that the buckets are made of food-grade plastic to prevent the leaching of harmful chemicals into the stored food. Additionally, verify that the lids create a tight seal to effectively keep out moisture and pests. For optimal food preservation, store the buckets in a cool and dry environment, similar to other storage containers.

Please keep in mind that certain foods are not well-suited for extended storage due to factors like moisture content, texture, or flavor preservation. These include fresh produce with high water content, such as watermelon or lettuce, and fresh dairy products like milk. Freshly baked goods, like bread, may also not store well long-term. Consider alternatives like powdered or evaporated milk and focus on dehydrated or freeze-dried fruits and vegetables.

By understanding the strengths and limitations of each storage container, you can effectively safeguard your long-term food supplies, ensuring they remain fresh and viable when you need them most.

Understanding Shelf Life and Planning for Long-Term Food Storage

Once you start preserving food, there are two questions you will face: How much food should you stock up on and how long will your ration last?

Tips on Planning

Effective planning is the backbone of a successful long-term food storage strategy. Here are some planning tips you can follow:

1. Family Members and Special Needs

Make a list of all family members and include any special needs such as allergies or medical conditions like diabetes. Tailor your food storage plan to accommodate these specific requirements.

2. Staple Foods Inventory

Take inventory of all staple foods on your shelves. Note the amount available, date of purchase or preserved, date opened, and any use-by or replace-by dates if known. This information serves as a reference for consumption and replenishment.

3. Freezer Inventory

Repeat the inventory process for foods in your freezer. Keep track of quantities, purchase dates, and any expiration dates. This step ensures you utilize frozen items before they lose quality.

4. Meal Preparation Notes

Adding notes to each day's list indicating water requirements, necessary equipment, and utensils for food preparation is a crucial planning step. This detailed approach prompts you to consider your needs thoroughly, which in turn facilitates efficient purchasing and storage.

5. Rotation of Non-Perishables

Keep your food supply fresh by implementing a rotation system for non-perishable items. Regularly rotate these staples in general storage, ensuring that older items are used first. This practice prevents waste and guarantees a reliable and up-to-date food inventory.

Shelf Life

Every food item has a finite shelf life, influenced by factors like packaging, storage conditions, and the type of food. Managing your food stockpile is key to maintaining a well-stocked and effective long-term food storage supply. Categorize foods based on their longevity, from canned goods with extended shelf lives to perishables with shorter durations.

By incorporating these tips into your planning process, you create a robust foundation for a well-organized, sustainable, and effective long-term food storage plan. This strategic approach enhances your preparedness for any unexpected situations that may arise.

LONG-TERM WATER STORAGE TIPS: PRESERVING THE ELIXIR OF LIFE

Water is a critical resource, and ensuring its safe storage and availability during emergencies is paramount. Let's dive into safe water storage methods, appropriate containers, and treatment options to guarantee a reliable and potable water supply in times of need.

One of the simplest and most convenient methods for storing water is through commercially available bottled water. Ensure bottles are made of food-grade materials and have not passed their expiration dates.

To provide for everyone's water needs, remember to have at least 1–2 gallons for each person for at least three days. If feasible, aim for a 2-week supply to enhance preparedness.

When preparing for emergency water storage, consider factors like choosing the right container, proper cleaning and sanitizing procedures, effective storage practices, and the appropriate use of stored water.

Choosing a Container

Opt for containers made from food-grade materials, such as high-density polyethylene (HDPE) or polyethylene terephthalate (PETE). These materials are safe for storing water and resistant to leaching harmful chemicals. Choose containers specifically designed for water storage by looking for those with tight-sealing lids or caps to prevent contamination and evaporation.

Consider the size of the container based on your storage needs. Larger containers are suitable for storing more significant amounts of water, but ensure they are manageable for handling and pouring. Transparent or semi-transparent containers allow you to monitor the water quality and easily check for any signs of contamination.

Ensure the container has a secure sealing mechanism. This prevents external contaminants, insects, or debris from entering the water. A tight seal also helps in preserving the water's freshness.

If possible, choose containers that are labeled as BPA-free. Bisphenol A (BPA) is a chemical found in some plastics and can leach into the water, posing health concerns.

Before storing water in the chosen container, it's crucial to clean and sanitize it properly to prevent contamination. Here's how to do it:

1. Wash the container with mild dish soap and water, removing any dirt or debris.
2. For narrow-necked containers, use a bottle brush to thoroughly clean hard-to-reach areas.
3. Rinse the container with clean water until all soap residue is removed.
4. Prepare a sanitizing solution by mixing one teaspoon of unscented liquid chlorine bleach per quart of water.
5. Pour the sanitizing solution into the container, ensuring all surfaces are coated.
6. Allow the sanitizing solution to sit in the container for at least two minutes to effectively kill any remaining bacteria or germs.
7. Drain the sanitizing solution from the container.
8. Let the container air dry completely before storing water in it to prevent any residual bleach from affecting the

water quality.

Storing the Water and Using Water

1. **Location:** Place water containers in a cool, dark area to prevent algae growth and maintain container integrity by avoiding sunlight exposure. Direct sunlight can encourage microbial growth and degrade stored water quality. Keep containers away from windows or any direct sunlight sources.
2. **Avoid Contaminants:** Keep water storage away from chemicals, solvents, or hazardous materials that could contaminate the water. Ensure containers are tightly sealed to prevent airborne contaminants, dust, or insects from entering.
3. **Rotation:** Regularly rotate stored water to ensure freshness, especially for long-term storage. Utilize the "first-in, first-out" (FIFO) method to consume older water first. Aim to rotate water at least every six months to prevent stagnation and maintain safety.
4. **Considerations:** Maintain consistent storage temperatures to preserve water taste and quality, avoiding extreme fluctuations. Elevate water containers to minimize ground contact and potential contamination.
5. **Monitoring:** Periodically inspect stored water for any signs of contamination, discoloration, or unusual odors, as well as their containers for wear, damage, or degradation. Replace containers that show signs of deterioration to maintain water quality.
6. **Emergency Preparedness:** Ensure stored water is easily accessible for emergencies, as quick access can be critical. Secure water storage areas to prevent spills or tampering.

When emergencies hit, it's important to be mindful of how we use our water for drinking and sanitation. Try to have at least a gallon of water per person per day for drinking and basic sanitation needs. Remember, your personal requirements may vary, so stay attuned to your body's signals. Drinking water should be at the top of the list, so staying hydrated is key for your well-being, especially during emergencies. Use reusable water bottles to measure your daily intake and make sure you're sipping steadily.

When it comes to sanitation, reserve some of your stored water for basic hygiene. Use it wisely for tasks like handwashing, simple cleaning, and, if necessary, flushing toilets. It's about finding that balance to make your water last. Conservation is the name of the game. Get creative with personal hygiene—wet wipes, hand sanitizers, and dry shampoos can be your allies. Think about using disposable plates and utensils to cut down on dishwashing. If you do have to wash, be mindful and use collected water efficiently.

When in a pinch, consider alternative water sources like melted ice from your freezer or water from your water heater (if it is safe to access). Keep an eye on your stored water quality, and if you're unsure, water purification tablets or filters can be handy.

Don't forget about your community. Reach out to neighbors and friends as sharing resources can make a significant difference for everyone. It's a team effort, after all. When it comes to children and the elderly, pay extra attention they may have specific needs, so adjust accordingly to ensure everyone's well taken care of.

Remember, staying informed, having a solid plan, and adapting your water usage to the situation will make a big impact on your overall well-being during emergencies.

Treatment Options for Contaminated Water

Boiling water is one of the simplest and most effective methods to clean contaminated water. Bring water to a rolling boil for at least one minute (or three minutes at higher altitudes) to kill the majority of pathogens, including bacteria, viruses, and parasites. Apart from boiling water, you can also make use of other methods.

Disinfection

Water disinfectant tablets or liquid are convenient options for eliminating harmful microorganisms. Follow the product's instructions carefully, as different disinfectants may have specific usage guidelines.

Chlorination

Adding chlorine bleach to water is a widely used method for disinfection. Ensure you follow specified guidelines for the correct concentration and contact time. This method is effective against a broad spectrum of pathogens.

Pasteurization

Pasteurization involves heating water to a specific temperature to eliminate pathogens without boiling. While not as common for individual use, it's a method employed on a larger scale in some situations.

Ultraviolet Radiation

UV light devices designed for water treatment are efficient in deactivating bacteria, viruses, and other microorganisms. These portable devices are suitable for purifying small quantities of water and are often used in camping or emergencies.

Filtration

Filtration offers a variety of methods to remove contaminants from water:

1. **Microfiltration:** This uses a fine mesh or ceramic filter to trap particles.
2. **Activated Carbon Filters:** These absorb impurities, chemicals, and organic substances.
3. **Oxidizing Filters:** These introduce oxygen to remove certain contaminants.
4. **Neutralizing Filters:** These adjust pH levels to make water less acidic or alkaline.
5. **Reverse Osmosis:** This forces water through a semi-permeable membrane to remove contaminants.
6. **Distillation:** This process involves heating water to create steam, which is then condensed back into liquid, leaving contaminants behind.

Choosing the appropriate filtration method depends on the specific contaminants present and the desired water quality.

Remember, the effectiveness of these methods can vary based on the type and extent of contamination. In critical situations, it's often advisable to use a combination of methods or seek professional guidance to ensure water safety.

Plato once said, "The greatest wealth is to live content with little" ("A Quote From Plato," n.d.). In the journey toward sustainable long-term food and water storage, this quote echoes the philosophy of being content with one's provisions. As we embark on this preparedness voyage, let the wisdom of prudent storage and mindful consumption guide our choices, ensuring our well-being in times of scarcity.

Planting a Seed for Someone Else's Tomorrow

What can you do today that can plant a seed for tomorrow?

— DEAN GRAZIOSI

Cast your mind back to the introduction, when I told you that only 39% of Americans have an emergency plan that their families are fully informed about. This is worrying enough on its own, but combine it with the fact the majority of people fear being unprepared for an emergency (a fear that's risen with the rise of natural disasters and pandemics in recent years), and it's clear that we have a problem.

You found this book because you realized how important it is to prepare your family for unpredictable emergencies, and I'm glad you did. The peace of mind you'll get from having a solid plan in place is unrivaled. Hopefully, you'll never have to fall back on that plan, but if you do, you'll know that you've done everything in your power to protect your family. You aren't the only one out there who was looking for this guidance. Of the thousands of people out there who know they're unprepared and are worried about it, many are looking for information to help them do something about it. I wrote this book with those people in mind, and now you've made it this far, I'd like to ask for your help in getting it to them.

That may sound like a lot, but helping other people begin their preparedness journey is one of the easiest things you'll do as part of your own quest. All you need to do is take a moment to leave a short review.

By leaving a review of this book on Amazon, you'll point anyone searching for this information in the right direction, and enable them to start building their plan.

Reviews help to connect people with the right resources, so while it may not seem like much to you, your words make a huge difference.

Thank you so much for your support. Of course, your family is your primary concern, but we're all in this together, and your support is truly valuable.

Leave a Review

MEDICAL SUPPLIES AND FIRST AID

 Healing is a matter of time, but it is sometimes also a matter of opportunity.

— HIPPOCRATES

These timeless words resonate profoundly as we delve into the critical chapter dedicated to assembling a comprehensive medical kit and understanding fundamental first aid techniques. This chapter is not just about acquiring supplies; it's about arming yourself with the knowledge to respond effectively in the face of medical emergencies.

Please note that I am not a medical professional, and the information provided in this chapter is for general educational purposes only. This chapter is not intended to provide specific medical advice, diagnosis, or treatment. It is important to consult a qualified healthcare professional for any medical concerns and to receive professional advice tailored to your specific health situation. Always seek the advice of a medical professional with any questions you may have regarding a medical condition, and never disregard professional medical advice or delay seeking it based on information in this book.

STOCKING A MEDICAL KIT

In the face of natural disasters or accidents, having emergency medical supplies and knowledge becomes even more critical. Immediate access to medical resources can be challenging during such events, making personal preparedness invaluable.

1. Plasters (various sizes and shapes): For covering minor cuts and abrasions.
2. Sterile Gauze Dressings (small, medium, and large): To dress wounds and promote healing.
3. Sterile Eye Dressings (at least two): For eye injuries or irritations.
4. Triangular Bandages: Versatile for creating slings or securing dressings.
5. Crêpe Rolled Bandages: Provides support for sprains and strains.
6. Safety Pins: To secure bandages and dressings.
7. Disposable Sterile Gloves: Maintains hygiene during first aid procedures.
8. Tweezers: For safely removing splinters or foreign objects.
9. Scissors: To cut tapes, bandages, or clothing in emergencies.
10. Alcohol-Free Cleansing Wipes: To cleanse wounds without irritating them.
11. Sticky Tape: Secures dressings and bandages in place.
12. Thermometer (digital preferred): Monitors body temperature for fever detection.

13. Skin Rash Cream (e.g., Hydrocortisone or Calendula): Soothes skin irritations.
14. Cream or Spray for Insect Bites and Stings: Provides relief from bites or stings.
15. Antiseptic Cream: Prevents infection in minor wounds.
16. Painkillers (Paracetamol, Aspirin, or Ibuprofen): Offers relief for pain and fever.
17. Antihistamine Cream or Tablets: Addresses allergic reactions.
18. Distilled Water: Ideal for cleaning wounds.
19. Eyewash and Eye Bath: Essential for eye care and emergencies.

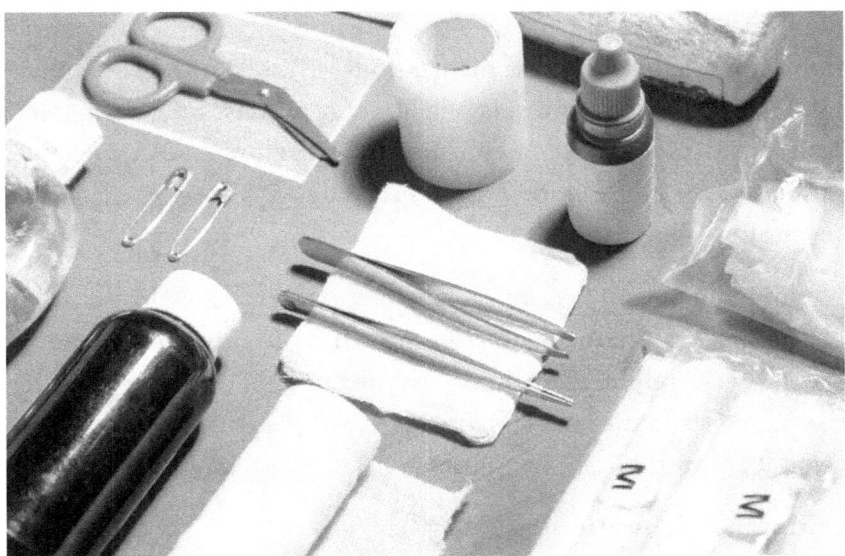

TAILORING THE KIT TO FAMILY HEALTH NEEDS

Customizing your family's medical kit is essential for ensuring preparedness for a variety of health needs. Consider the following aspects to tailor your kit effectively:

Prescription Medications:

Take inventory of any specific health conditions within your family that require prescription medications. Ensure that an adequate supply of these medications is stored in the kit, considering the duration of potential emergencies.

Allergies and Chronic Conditions:

Identify family members with allergies or chronic health conditions, and include relevant medications or tools in the emergency kit. For individuals with severe allergic reactions, such as anaphylaxis, ensure you have epinephrine auto-injectors readily available. Similarly, for those with asthma, include inhalers for managing respiratory symptoms.

For individuals with more serious respiratory issues like chronic obstructive pulmonary disease (COPD), consider including specialized equipment such as a nebulizer. A nebulizer is a device that converts liquid medicine into a mist for inhalation, providing relief from respiratory symptoms.

Children's Medications:

If you have children, ensure the inclusion of age-appropriate medications and dosages in the kit. Pediatric formulations of painkillers and fever reducers are crucial additions to address common childhood ailments.

Individual Health Considerations:

Take into account any unique health needs or requirements of family members. Include specific over-the-counter medications or medical devices based on individual health profiles.

Specialized Equipment:

For family members requiring specialized equipment, ensure that the kit includes these items. Examples include oxygen tanks, crutches, wheelchairs, or any other medical devices necessary for mobility or daily living. Familiarize yourself with the proper use and maintenance of such equipment to ensure readiness during emergencies.

It's important to emphasize that a well-stocked medical kit is a fundamental aspect of household preparedness. Make sure to routinely inspect and replenish the contents of the kit to ensure that all supplies are within their expiration dates. Being ready for a range of health situations allows for quick and effective responses to medical needs within the family.

ESSENTIAL MEDICATION AND THEIR USES

Having a basic understanding of the essential medicines and knowing how to use them is important for several reasons:

1. Immediate Relief

Pain relievers like Acetaminophen, Aspirin, Ibuprofen, and Naproxen provide quick relief from pain and fever. Knowing when and how to use them can offer immediate relief in various situations.

2. Managing Common Ailments

Medications for heartburn and indigestion (Omeprazole, Lansoprazole, Cimetidine, Aluminium Hydroxide), laxatives (Bisacodyl, Calcium Docusate), and antidiarrheal drugs (Bismuth Subsalicylate, Loperamide) help manage common gastrointestinal issues that can arise unexpectedly.

3. Preventing Motion Sickness

Motion sickness medication such as Dimenhydrinate is vital, particularly during travel. Understanding how to use it can help prevent and alleviate symptoms like nausea, vomiting, and dizziness associated with motion sickness.

4. Addressing Respiratory Issues

Respiratory issues, including asthma, require specialized attention in emergency preparedness. Alongside nasal steroids like Fluticasone and Triamcinolone and cough medicines like Guaifenesin, it's crucial to include medications specifically targeted at managing asthma symptoms.

Rescue Inhalers, such as Albuterol Sulfate, play a vital role in managing acute asthma symptoms like wheezing, chest tightness, and shortness of breath. These inhalers provide quick relief by relaxing the muscles in the airways, facilitating easier breathing during asthma attacks. Their rapid action makes them indispensable for alleviating sudden exacerbations and swiftly restoring normal breathing patterns.

On the other hand, controller medications serve as long-term management tools for asthma symptoms. These include inhaled corticosteroids like Fluticasone and long-acting beta-agonists such as Salmeterol. By incorporating controller medications into your emergency kit, you ensure ongoing asthma management, even during prolonged emergencies. These medications help prevent flare-ups and maintain optimal respiratory function over extended periods.

Nebulizers are indispensable for individuals with severe asthma or those unable to use inhalers effectively. Nebulizers offer an alternative delivery method for asthma medication, ensuring effective treatment for individuals with diverse needs.

Aside from medication, it's essential to monitor asthma symptoms closely. A peak flow meter, a handheld device, is used to gauge the effectiveness of air movement out of the lungs. Through regular monitoring of peak flow readings, individuals can evaluate the severity of their asthma symptoms and monitor their lung function's progression.

Lastly, including a written asthma action plan in your emergency kit is essential. This plan outlines step-by-step instructions for managing asthma exacerbations, including medication dosages, emergency contact information, and steps for seeking medical assistance if symptoms worsen. A well-prepared asthma action plan ensures a prompt and effective response to asthma attacks, enhancing overall asthma management and improving outcomes during emergencies.

5. Allergy Management

Antihistamines (Fexofenadine, Loratadine) help alleviate allergy symptoms, including sneezing and itching. Being familiar with their use is beneficial for those prone to allergies.

6. Skincare

Emollients and mild corticosteroid creams are essential for managing skin conditions. Understanding their application helps soothe and treat skin irritations, inflammation, and itching.

7. Antibiotics for Bacterial Infections

Antibiotics are crucial for treating bacterial infections. Knowing when to use them and completing the full course as prescribed by a healthcare professional is vital to ensure effective treatment and prevent antibiotic resistance.

8. Caution With Antivirals

Antivirals like Ivermectin and Acyclovir are used in specific conditions. However, their use is controversial, and guidance from a healthcare professional is essential. Understanding their appropriate use is crucial for addressing viral infections.

Additionally, you can communicate with your physicians about your intention to keep extra medication stocked in case of a natural disaster. Discussing this with your healthcare provider ensures that they are aware of your preparedness efforts and can offer valuable advice on how to safely store and maintain a stock of necessary medications.

During these conversations, your physician can guide you on

1. proper storage conditions for different medications to maintain their effectiveness.
2. recommendations for rotating medications to ensure that you use the oldest medicines first, following the FIFO (First In, First Out) principle.

3. any specific considerations or precautions regarding the storage of certain medications, such as temperature sensitivity or shelf life.

Many physicians understand the need for emergency prepared-ness and can offer personalized advice based on your medical history and needs. By involving your healthcare provider in your preparedness plans, you can ensure that your family's medical kit is well-maintained and ready to use when needed. Remember to regularly review and update your emergency supplies in consulta-tion with your physician to keep them current and effective.

Guidelines on Safe Storage and Expiry Dates

Safe Storage:

- Store medication in a cool, dry place away from direct sunlight.
- Keep them out of reach of children and pets.
- Follow storage instructions on the medication packaging.

Expiry Dates:

- Regularly check and monitor expiry dates on medications.
- Do not use medication that has passed its expiration date, as it may be ineffective or even harmful.

In summary, having and knowing how to use these essential medi-cines provides you with a toolkit to address common health issues and emergencies. However, it's crucial to use them responsibly, following prescribed dosages and seeking professional advice when needed. Additionally, staying informed about storage condi-tions and expiry dates ensures the effectiveness and safety of these medications. It's always advisable to consult with a healthcare professional for personalized guidance on medication use.

BASIC FIRST AID TECHNIQUES AND TRAINING

Medical emergencies can be stressful. Learn strategies to maintain composure and clear thinking when faced with challenging situations. A calm demeanor can significantly impact the effectiveness of your response. Consider enrolling in basic first aid and CPR courses because acquiring the knowledge and hands-on experience provided by certified instructors enhances your ability to administer aid confidently and effectively.

1. Cuts

A. Clean the wound: Wash your hands and then the wound with mild soap and water.
B. Apply pressure: Use a clean cloth or sterile bandage to control bleeding.
C. Elevate the injury: If possible, raise the injured part to reduce blood flow.

2. Burns

A. Cool the burn: Hold the affected area under cool (not cold) running water for at least 10 minutes.
B. Protect the burn: Cover the burn with a sterile non-stick bandage or clean cloth.
C. Take pain relief: Over-the-counter pain relievers can be used for pain management.

3. Sprains

   A. Rest the injured area: Avoid putting weight on the affected limb.
   B. Ice: Apply an ice pack to the injured area for 15–20 minutes every 2–3 hours.
   C. Compression: Use a compression bandage to reduce swelling.
   D. Elevation: Keep the injured area elevated to minimize swelling.

4. Fractures

   A. Immobilize the limb: Keep the injured limb as still as possible, using a splint or other support.
   B. Apply ice: Use ice to reduce pain and swelling.
   C. Seek medical help: Call for professional assistance immediately.

5. Choking

   A. Encourage coughing: If someone is coughing forcefully, encourage them to keep coughing.
   B. Perform the Heimlich maneuver: If the person can't cough, perform abdominal thrusts.
   C. Call for emergency help: If the obstruction persists, call for professional assistance.

Important Note: Taking a certified first aid and CPR course that covers the Heimlich maneuver is highly recommended for individuals of all ages and backgrounds. These courses provide comprehensive instruction on recognizing and responding to various medical emergencies, including choking incidents. By participating in such training programs, you gain hands-on experience in performing the Heimlich maneuver on both adults and children under the guidance of qualified instructors.

Importance of Formal First Aid Training

Formal first aid training not only boosts your confidence in handling emergencies but also ensures you're proficient in assessing situations and administering aid effectively. This training covers a broad spectrum of scenarios, guiding you from basic injuries to critical and life-threatening situations. It offers in-depth knowledge on responding appropriately to various emergencies.

Think of it this way: In those crucial moments, before professional help arrives, your knowledge gained from first aid training can be the difference between a positive outcome and a more challenging situation. You'll be equipped not only to act promptly but also to tailor your responses based on the specific needs of the situation, considering factors like age, health conditions, and the environment.

Here's the bonus: Holding formal first aid certification can provide you with legal protection in certain situations. In many places, being trained in first aid can shield you from legal liabilities when you're assisting in emergencies.

A community where more people are trained in first aid becomes a safer place because a trained group can collectively respond to emergencies, contributing to the overall safety and well-being of everyone.

Signing up for formal first aid training is an investment toward your ability to respond effectively during emergencies. It provides you with the necessary skills and knowledge to make a meaningful impact in critical situations. Explore options from local organizations, community centers, or online platforms offering accredited first aid courses. Always keep in mind that being prepared can make a significant difference when it matters the most.

As we embark on the journey toward preparing medical essentials for whatever disaster may strike, let's draw inspiration from the timeless wisdom found in Jeremiah 33:6: "Behold, I will bring it health and cure, and I will cure them and will reveal unto them the abundance of peace and truth" (*King James Bible*, 2024c).

This scripture encapsulates the profound connection between health and healing. It reminds us that the pursuit of well-being is not only a physical endeavor but also a journey that encompasses the richness of peace and truth.

As we explore ways to care for ourselves and our families, let this scripture serve as a guiding light, emphasizing the holistic nature of healing. May our efforts toward preparedness be infused with the promise of abundance in peace and truth, creating a harmonious balance that extends beyond the physical realm.

Now, with this guiding principle, let's continue our exploration of knowledge and practices to be better prepared for emergencies.

FINANCIAL PREPAREDNESS

> *For which of you, intending to build a tower, sitteth not down first, and counteth the cost, whether he have sufficient to finish it?*

— LUKE 14:28 (KJV)

Luke 14:28 beautifully encapsulates the wisdom of planning and foresight. Financial preparedness is not just about managing day-to-day expenses but also about building resilience for unforeseen circumstances. In this chapter, we'll delve into strategies for budgeting, saving, and managing finances to ensure stability during emergencies. By adopting proactive financial habits, you can safeguard yourself and your loved ones against financial hardships that may arise during times of crisis.

Let's explore practical ways to strengthen your financial foundation and navigate uncertainties with confidence. Whether it's creating a robust budget, establishing an emergency fund, or making informed investment decisions, the principles of financial preparedness outlined in this chapter will empower you to weather life's storms and emerge stronger.

STRATEGIES FOR FINANCIAL STABILITY IN CRISES

Having an emergency fund offers numerous benefits that contribute to overall financial well-being. Firstly, it provides a sense of financial security by serving as a buffer against unexpected expenses. Building up this reserve diminishes the necessity of depending on credit cards or loans, thus mitigating the risk of accumulating debt over time. By having funds readily available for emergencies, individuals can navigate financial challenges with greater ease and confidence.

Furthermore, an emergency fund serves as a key factor in reducing stress. Having the assurance of funds set aside specifically for unforeseen circumstances alleviates the stress and anxiety linked with financial uncertainty. This peace of mind empowers you to concentrate on finding solutions rather than fretting about how to manage unexpected expenses.

Additionally, with savings in place, there's less reliance on borrowing money to cover sudden costs. This reduces the risk of accumulating high-interest debt, which can have long-term implications for financial health. By prioritizing savings, you can maintain greater financial stability and resilience in the face of unexpected events.

Furthermore, an emergency fund opens up opportunities for seizing potential benefits during challenging times. Having savings on hand allows you to capitalize on opportunities that may arise, such as investing in education or starting a business. This financial flexibility empowers us to make strategic decisions and pursue avenues for personal and professional growth, even in times of uncertainty.

The significance of an emergency fund cannot be emphasized enough. From providing financial security and reducing stress to avoiding debt and seizing opportunities, an emergency fund serves as a cornerstone of sound financial planning and resilience. By prioritizing savings and building a robust emergency fund, individuals can better navigate life's uncertainties and achieve greater financial peace of mind.

Creating an emergency fund is a foundational aspect of financial planning, requiring intentional effort and disciplined savings habits. Here are some strategies you can implement:

1. Set a Savings Goal

Setting a clear savings goal is the initial step in creating an emergency fund. Calculate the amount required to cover emergencies, targeting at least three to six months' worth of living expenses. It's crucial to adapt this goal according to your specific circumstances, including family size, income stability, and career outlook.

2. Track Expenses

Monitoring your monthly expenses is crucial for identifying areas where you can cut back or eliminate unnecessary spending. Reviewing your spending habits allows you to redirect these funds toward your emergency fund, accelerating its growth. Utilize budgeting tools or apps to track expenses effectively and gain insights into your spending patterns.

3. Start Small

Begin your savings journey by setting achievable goals, even if they initially seem modest. Consistency is key, so start by allocating a small percentage of your income to your emergency fund—every dollar contributes to building financial resilience over time. As your financial situation improves, gradually increase your savings contributions to reach your target goal.

4. Automate Savings

Automating your savings is a potent strategy for maintaining consistency and discipline in growing your emergency fund. Arrange automatic transfers from your chequing account to your emergency fund at regular intervals, whether monthly or with each paycheck. By automating your savings, you eliminate the temptation to spend impulsively and establish saving as a habitual practice.

5. Prioritize Savings

Regard your emergency fund as a non-negotiable expense, prioritizing it above discretionary spending. Establish saving as a habit by integrating it into your budget and financial plan from the beginning. By viewing your emergency fund as a critical component of financial security, you instill the discipline needed to consistently achieve your savings goals.

6. Use Windfalls Wisely

Redirecting unexpected windfalls, such as tax refunds or bonuses, toward your emergency fund can accelerate its growth. Instead of splurging on non-essential purchases, view windfalls as opportunities to strengthen your financial safety net. By using windfalls wisely, you expedite your progress toward achieving your emergency fund target.

7. Review and Adjust

Periodically review your savings progress and adjust your goals as needed to stay on track. Life circumstances may change, such as changes in income, expenses, or family dynamics, necessitating a reassessment of your emergency fund target. Be flexible and adaptable in your approach, making adjustments as required to ensure continued financial resilience.

By following these steps and adopting a proactive approach to building an emergency fund, you can strengthen your financial security and readiness to face unforeseen challenges with confidence. Consistent saving habits, coupled with prudent financial management, lay the foundation for a robust emergency fund that provides peace of mind and stability in times of need.

Diversifying Income

Diversifying income for emergency preparedness can be a financial safety move when unexpected situations arise. It's all about spreading your income sources across different avenues to ensure that you're not solely reliant on one stream of revenue. This strategy not only enhances your financial security but also helps to cushion the impact of any unforeseen events or emergencies. Let's have a look at some of the ways you can diversify your income. Of course, you should choose options that suit your needs and financial abilities.

Stock Market

Investing in the stock market is a widely adopted method for individuals to increase their wealth. It offers the chance for capital appreciation and dividends, which drive investment returns. Capital appreciation happens when investments increase in value over time due to company growth and profitability. Dividends are portions of a company's earnings distributed to shareholders, providing passive income.

Indeed, stock market investing carries risks such as market volatility and potential losses. To navigate these risks effectively, investors must conduct thorough research and analysis before making decisions. This involves assessing economic conditions, company fundamentals, industry trends, and market sentiment. Understanding these factors enables investors to make informed choices aligned with their financial goals and risk tolerance levels.

Diversification plays a pivotal role in stock market investing. By spreading investments across various companies, industries, and asset classes, investors can mitigate the impact of adverse events on any single investment. Diversification helps reduce risk and stabilize portfolio returns over time.

Successful stock market investing often requires a long-term perspective. Though short-term fluctuations occur, historical data shows that the market tends to trend upward over time. Thus, staying disciplined and invested for the long haul can lead to favorable outcomes. Effective risk management strategies, like setting clear investment goals, diversifying portfolios, and reviewing holdings regularly, are essential for navigating uncertainties and achieving long-term financial success.

Stock market investing presents opportunities for wealth accumulation but demands careful consideration, research, and risk management. By grasping investing principles, diversifying portfolios, and adopting a long-term outlook, individuals can leverage the stock market's potential to reach financial goals and build wealth over time.

REITs (Real Estate Investment Trusts)

Real estate investment trusts (REITs) provide a convenient avenue for investing in real estate without the need to own property directly. By investing in REITs, individuals can participate in a diverse portfolio of real estate assets alongside other investors, without the burdens associated with property management.

REITs allow investment in various real estate sectors like commercial buildings, residential complexes, shopping centers, and hotels, offering exposure to the market through publicly traded shares. One key advantage is diversification which spreads your investment across different properties and locations to reduce risk.

Unlike traditional real estate investments, REITs provide liquidity as they are traded on stock exchanges. This means you can easily buy and sell shares, accessing your investment when needed. Additionally, REITs offer income potential through dividends, providing a steady cash flow alongside potential capital appreciation.

Managed by experienced professionals, REITs handle property acquisition, management, leasing, and disposition, aiming to maximize performance and shareholder value. With benefits like diversification, liquidity, income generation, and growth potential, REITs offer a valuable option for long-term wealth accumulation without the hassles of property ownership. Consider exploring REITs to diversify and potentially grow your investment portfolio.

Online Opportunities

Unlock your potential and capitalize on online opportunities to share your knowledge, interests, and expertise with the world. Whether through vlogging, blogging, podcasting, or affiliate marketing, digital platforms offer unmatched scalability and flexibility to monetize your content creation efforts according to your lifestyle and passions.

Vlogging is perfect for those who enjoy sharing life experiences, hobbies, or expertise through video. Dive into topics like travel, cooking, gaming, fitness, or beauty, and build a loyal following to monetize through ad revenue, sponsored content, merchandise sales, or brand partnerships.

For those with a way with words, blogging provides a platform to share valuable information or storytelling on niche expertise, hobbies, or observations. Monetize your blog through advertising, sponsored content, affiliate marketing, digital products, or exclusive memberships.

Podcasting offers a route for storytelling, interviewing, or sharing insights through audio. With a vast audience hungry for engaging content, explore niche topics, interview experts, or share personal stories while making money through sponsorships, advertising, listener donations, or premium content.

Affiliate marketing is ideal for those passionate about recommending products or services they believe in. Partner with companies and earn commissions for sales or referrals, whether through product reviews, tutorials, or recommendations.

Embrace the world of online opportunities, whether through videos, articles, audio, or product recommendations. With dedication and creativity, transform your online endeavors into a fulfilling and profitable income stream.

Consulting

Consider harnessing your professional expertise through consulting—a fulfilling career path where you can offer valuable guidance to businesses or individuals. Consulting encompasses a wide array of services, from advice and problem-solving to strategic direction, tailored to meet client needs.

Specialize in areas where you excel, such as management, finance, marketing, technology, healthcare, or legal services, and help clients overcome challenges and achieve their objectives. Engagements can vary in duration and scope, from short-term projects to long-term partnerships, offering flexibility in how you work.

Clients benefit from your specialized knowledge and unbiased assessments, gaining innovative solutions and actionable recommendations. By closely aligning with client goals, you drive business growth and improve performance, making a tangible impact on their success.

While consulting is rewarding, it comes with challenges like managing client expectations and maintaining a work-life balance. Success requires strong communication, problem-solving, and project management skills, along with staying updated on industry trends and technologies.

Overall, consulting offers opportunities for continuous learning and professional growth, allowing you to make a meaningful impact while building a fulfilling and lucrative career. Consider leveraging your expertise to embark on this rewarding journey.

Coaching

Coaching services provide a potent method for guiding clients toward their personal or professional aspirations. Whether it's career advancement, health enhancement, or personal development, coaching empowers individuals with the tools and strategies needed for success.

As a coach, you collaborate closely with clients to pinpoint their goals, surmount obstacles, and unlock their potential. Through personalized one-on-one sessions, you assist clients in establishing goals, crafting action plans, and monitoring progress over time, fostering clarity, confidence, and substantial advancement.

One of coaching's strengths is its personalized approach that focuses on the present and future to create actionable strategies for progress. By providing accountability and support, coaches empower clients to make positive changes and realize their full potential.

Coaching comes in various forms, including executive, career, life, and health coaching, each offering opportunities to use your expertise and passion to make a difference. Beyond individual coaching, you can expand your reach through group programs, workshops, or online courses, reaching a wider audience and simultaneously providing support to multiple clients.

Ultimately, coaching is about unlocking inner greatness and helping individuals live their best lives. By becoming a coach, you can inspire, motivate, and empower others to achieve their goals and create lasting positive change. If you're passionate about making a difference, coaching could be the perfect path for you.

Freelancing

Freelancing provides unmatched flexibility and independence, allowing individuals to offer services on a contract basis without traditional employment constraints. Whether you're a writer, a designer, a programmer, or skilled in any field, freelancing lets you showcase your talents worldwide.

As a freelancer, you have the freedom to choose clients, set rates, and define your schedule, working from anywhere. This flexibility enables a work-life balance tailored to your needs. Freelancing also diversifies skills and portfolios, offering projects aligned with interests and career goals.

A significant advantage of freelancing is its unlimited earning potential. Income correlates with skills, reputation, and results. With dedication, freelancers can command higher rates, attract premium clients, and build thriving businesses.

Freelancing fosters personal and professional growth through diverse projects, expanding networks, and valuable experiences. Yet, it requires self-discipline, time management, and financial planning. Despite challenges, freelancing offers a rewarding career for those passionate about their craft, seeking independence, and embracing creative opportunities.

Side Hustles

Side hustles are extra income-generating activities pursued alongside your main job. They offer flexibility and rewards, allowing you to boost earnings, explore interests, or save for goals.

These side gigs vary widely, from driving for ride-sharing services or selling crafts online to renting out property on platforms like Airbnb. They let you leverage your skills and interests to create additional income streams on your terms.

Side hustles provide autonomy to fit around your schedule and lifestyle, whether you have a few spare hours weekly or prefer weekend work. Besides extra income, they offer personal and professional fulfillment, allowing you to pursue passions and develop new skills.

However, it's crucial to manage side hustles realistically and balance them with other commitments to avoid burnout. While they can be lucrative and enjoyable, they require time, effort, and dedication to succeed.

Overall, side hustles offer a unique chance to diversify income, pursue passions, and take control of financial futures. Whether you're aiming for extra cash or wanting to explore new interests, starting a side hustle can be rewarding and empowering.

Selling Merchandise

Selling merchandise, whether branded products or digital downloads, can be a lucrative venture, especially for influencers or content creators with a loyal following. Developing merchandise enables you to utilize your audience and brand identity to generate additional revenue. Whether you're a YouTuber, podcaster, or social media influencer, merchandise provides fans with a tangible means to support and connect with your content.

One benefit of selling merchandise is its scalability and passive income potential. Once launched, products can continue to generate revenue passively, providing financial stability and freedom.

Selling merchandise also strengthens your brand and increases visibility. Branded items serve as free advertising and foster a sense of community among your audience.

Strategically approach selling merchandise by understanding your audience. Create products that align with your brand, and promote them through various channels.

In summary, selling merchandise is a fantastic way to monetize your brand, engage with your audience, and diversify your income streams, resulting in a profitable and rewarding venture.

Creating Courses

Developing and selling online courses on platforms like Udemy or Teachable presents an excellent opportunity to monetize your expertise while aiding others in learning and development. Courses cover a wide array of subjects, from professional skills to hobbies, drawing in eager learners.

Creating online courses enables you to impart your knowledge and best practices in an easily accessible format, catering to learners of all proficiency levels. The scalability and potential for passive income are significant advantages, offering financial stability as courses continue to passively generate revenue.

Furthermore, creating courses positions you as an authority in your field, expanding your network and fostering opportunities for collaboration. However, strategic planning is essential. Research to understand your audience's needs, invest in high-quality content production, and promote your courses effectively to attract students. Developing and selling online courses is a fulfilling way to share knowledge, assist others, and establish a sustainable business. Whether you're seeking to monetize your expertise or diversify your income streams, online courses present valuable opportunities for growth and achievement.

Cryptocurrency

Cryptocurrency, a digital currency operating on decentralized networks through blockchain technology, has garnered attention for its potential returns and innovative features. Investing or trading in cryptocurrencies provides profit opportunities, with notable examples like Bitcoin witnessing significant value surges. However, caution is warranted due to the high volatility and inherent risks associated with the cryptocurrency market.

Cryptocurrency markets are speculative and prone to extreme fluctuations, resulting in substantial gains or losses. To manage risks effectively, conducting thorough research and due diligence is essential. Gain a comprehensive understanding of blockchain fundamentals, market drivers, and trends. Practice discipline and implement risk management strategies by diversifying your portfolio and investing only what you can afford to lose.

Establish clear goals and strategies to mitigate emotional responses to market fluctuations. Security risks, including hacking and scams, are prevalent in the cryptocurrency space. Utilize reputable exchanges and wallets, employ robust security measures such as two-factor authentication, and remain vigilant against fraudulent activities.

Despite the risks involved, cryptocurrency offers potential gains and the opportunity for portfolio diversification for those willing to navigate the volatility. Stay informed, exercise caution, and adopt a disciplined approach to capitalize on growth opportunities while minimizing risks.

Writing a Book

Writing a book, whether fiction or non-fiction, allows for creative expression and a lasting impact on readers. With various genres to explore, such as novels, memoirs, or self-help guides, the possibilities are endless.

One significant benefit is the potential for passive income through royalties, providing ongoing earnings post-publication. Self-publishing platforms like Amazon Kindle Direct Publishing (KDP) make it accessible to reach a global audience.

Beyond income, writing a book establishes authority in your field, opening doors to speaking engagements and media appearances. It's a fulfilling experience where you get to share your insights and leave a legacy.

Approach with dedication, patience, and discipline, crafting compelling narratives and refining your manuscript. Start by brainstorming ideas, outlining, and setting realistic goals. Seek feedback and embrace the journey, celebrating milestones along the way.

Whether seasoned or new, writing a book offers a rewarding opportunity to share your voice and impact the world.

Dropshipping

Dropshipping entails selling products online without inventory, as suppliers fulfill orders directly. This model frees up time for marketing and customer service.

Diversifying income with strategies like dropshipping, investing, freelancing, or online courses offers stability and growth opportunities. Spreading income reduces dependency and safeguards against economic changes. Evaluate each opportunity based on risk, time, and returns. Some yield quick results with minimal effort, while others require more investment.

Though building multiple income streams takes effort, the benefits are significant. It provides financial security, flexibility, and personal growth opportunities.

Diversifying income through a combination of these strategies can provide stability, resilience, and opportunities for growth in varying economic conditions. It's essential to evaluate each opportunity carefully, considering factors such as risk tolerance, time commitment, and potential returns. By building multiple income streams, individuals can better navigate financial challenges and achieve greater financial security.

BUDGETING AND SAVING TIPS FOR EMERGENCIES

When it comes to preparing for emergencies, budgeting and saving are key components of financial resilience. Firstly, break down your savings goals into smaller, more manageable steps. Setting realistic targets makes it easier to track progress and stay motivated along the way. Whether it's saving a certain amount each month or reaching a specific savings milestone, breaking it down can make the process less daunting.

Consider opening a separate emergency savings account. Having a dedicated account specifically for emergencies helps you avoid dipping into your regular savings for non-urgent expenses. Plus, it adds a layer of organization and clarity to your financial goals.

Automating deposits into your emergency savings account is another effective strategy. By setting up automatic transfers from your chequing account to your savings account, you ensure that a portion of your income is consistently allocated toward emergency savings without having to manually transfer funds each time. You could also arrange with your employer to have a certain percentage or fixed amount of your earnings automatically transferred to your emergency savings account every payday. This way, you're effectively paying yourself first for any unexpected expenses or rainy days that may come your way. Most employers offer direct deposit as a convenient option for employees who receive their pay electronically. By taking advantage of this service, you eliminate the need to remember to transfer money manually. I personally swear by this method because, let's face it, when money is out of sight, it's out of mind. By diverting a portion of my paycheck directly into my emergency savings, I'm less tempted to spend it on unnecessary purchases. It's a simple yet powerful way to build up your financial safety net over time.

Additionally, whenever you come across extra money, whether it's a bonus, tax refund, or unexpected windfall, consider funneling it into your emergency savings account. This allows you to accelerate your savings progress without impacting your regular budget.

To boost your savings further, look for ways to increase your income and cut unnecessary expenses. Whether it's taking on a side hustle, negotiating a raise, or trimming discretionary spending, every little bit counts toward building your emergency fund.

In addition to these budgeting and saving tips, consider adopting the 50/30/20 budgeting method to achieve your financial goals. This approach allocates 50% of your income toward needs (such as housing, utilities, and groceries), 30% toward wants (such as dining out, entertainment, and travel), and 20% toward savings and debt repayment.

Another budgeting method to consider is the zero-based budget. With this approach, every dollar of your income is allocated toward specific categories, such as bills, savings, and expenses, until you've reached zero. This method encourages you to give every dollar a job and ensures that you're fully aware of where your money is going.

By incorporating these budgeting and saving tips into your financial plan, you can build a solid foundation for handling emergencies and achieving your long-term financial goals. Remember, financial preparedness is about taking proactive steps to protect yourself and your loved ones, and budgeting and saving are essential tools in your toolkit.

MONEY MATTERS DURING DISASTERS

When it comes to preparing for natural disasters, financial readiness is just as crucial as physical preparedness. Firstly, ensure that all your important financial documents are backed up digitally on a thumb drive or stored securely in the cloud. This includes insurance policies, identification documents, bank account information, and any other essential paperwork. Having digital copies ensures that you can access these documents even if the originals are damaged or lost during a disaster.

Next, create a visual inventory of your valuables by taking photos or videos of your possessions. This documentation can be invaluable when filing insurance claims after a disaster and helps ensure that you receive adequate compensation for any losses.

Consider setting up a safety-net savings account specifically earmarked for emergencies. Aim to gradually build up this fund over time, allocating a portion of your income toward it regularly. Having a dedicated emergency savings account provides a financial buffer in case of unexpected expenses or loss of income.

In addition to savings, it's wise to keep some cash on hand in case of emergencies. During natural disasters, power outages and disruptions to banking services may make electronic payments inaccessible, so having cash readily available can help you cover immediate expenses like food, water, and transportation.

It's also a good idea to keep a credit card or other financial tool for emergencies. While cash is essential, having access to additional funds through credit can provide extra financial flexibility when needed.

To ensure that your essential bills continue to be paid on time, consider setting up auto payments for important expenses like rent, mortgage, utilities, and insurance premiums. This helps prevent missed payments, late fees, and potential service interruptions during emergencies.

Additionally, it's crucial to routinely assess your insurance coverage to guarantee sufficient protection against a variety of disasters. This encompasses homeowners or renters insurance, flood insurance, earthquake insurance, and any other pertinent policies. Make any required updates or modifications to your coverage in response to changes in your circumstances or risk factors.

Finally, consider having your roof inspected regularly to identify and address any potential vulnerabilities or damage that could worsen during a natural disaster. A well-maintained roof can help minimize the risk of water damage and structural issues during severe weather events.

In conclusion, careful financial planning is essential for weathering the financial impact of natural disasters. By taking proactive steps to prepare your finances, you can minimize the stress and financial strain associated with emergencies and increase your resilience in the face of adversity.

As Warren Buffett wisely said, "Do not save what is left after spending, but spend what is left after saving" ("A Quote by Warren Buffett," n.d.). This quote emphasizes the importance of prioritizing savings and prudent financial management, especially in uncertain times. By adopting a mindset of proactive saving and careful financial planning, you can build a solid foundation for financial security and peace of mind, even in the face of unexpected challenges.

SPECIAL CONSIDERATIONS: CHILDREN, PETS, AND THE ELDERLY

 The true measure of any society can be found in how it treats its most vulnerable members.

— MAHATMA GANDHI

In times of emergency, it's essential to ensure that all family members, including children, pets, and the elderly, are adequately cared for and included in emergency preparedness plans. This chapter focuses on integrating and engaging every member of the family in preparedness activities to ensure their safety and well-being during crises.

Children, with their unique needs and vulnerabilities, require special consideration when planning for emergencies. It's crucial to involve them in preparedness activities in age-appropriate ways, such as teaching them about emergency procedures, practicing drills together, and providing reassurance and comfort during stressful situations. Additionally, parents should ensure that emergency kits include essential items like diapers, formula, medications, comfort items, and games or activities to keep children occupied and calm during emergencies.

Pets are beloved members of the family and should not be overlooked when creating emergency plans. It's essential to include provisions for their care and safety in the event of a disaster. This includes ensuring that they have identification tags, microchips, and up-to-date vaccinations, as well as packing a pet emergency kit with food, water, medications, leashes, carriers, and bedding. Families should also identify pet-friendly shelters or accommodations in case of evacuation and have a plan for how to evacuate pets safely.

Elderly family members may have specific health concerns or mobility issues that need to be addressed in emergency plans. As a caregiver, it's crucial to make sure that emergency kits are stocked with all essential medications, medical supplies, mobility aids, and assistive devices. It's also essential to establish communication and evacuation plans that consider the unique needs of elderly family members, such as arranging for transportation or assistance from neighbors or caregivers if necessary.

By including children, pets, and elderly family members in emergency preparedness planning, families can ensure that everyone is accounted for and provided for during crises. Taking proactive steps to address their needs and vulnerabilities demonstrates a commitment to caring for all members of the family and reinforces the strength and resilience of the family unit in the face of adversity.

PREPAREDNESS FOR CHILDREN

Involving children in emergency plans is crucial to ensuring their safety and well-being during crises. By addressing their unique needs and vulnerabilities and empowering them with knowledge and skills, parents can help children feel more secure and prepared in the face of emergencies.

Starting open and age-appropriate discussions about emergencies and safety is crucial for empowering children with the knowledge and confidence to respond effectively during uncertain situations. Using simple language and offering reassurance, parents and caregivers can create a safe space for children to express their concerns and ask questions. By emphasizing that they are safe and cared for, adults can help alleviate any fears or anxieties children may have about emergencies.

Teaching children how to recognize emergencies and take appropriate action is an essential aspect of preparedness. Educating them on staying calm, identifying trusted adults, and seeking shelter can empower children to respond calmly and confidently during crises. Through ongoing conversations and role-playing scenarios, children can develop the skills and awareness needed to navigate emergencies with resilience and resourcefulness.

Regularly practicing emergency drills is a practical way to familiarize children with evacuation procedures and safety protocols. Making drills fun and interactive can help reduce anxiety and reinforce learning. By incorporating games, challenges, or rewards, parents can engage children in the process and turn emergency preparedness into a positive and empowering experience.

Involving children in the creation of a family emergency kit is another valuable opportunity to teach preparedness skills and foster a sense of ownership. By allowing children to select items like snacks, games, and comfort items to include in the kit, parents can help them feel actively involved in the preparedness process. This collaborative approach not only reinforces the importance of emergency planning but also strengthens family bonds and resilience.

Utilizing storytelling, role-playing, or games to teach children about emergency preparedness concepts adds an element of fun and engagement to the learning process. Through imaginative play and interactive activities, children can learn about fire safety, severe weather awareness, basic first aid, and other essential topics memorably and enjoyably. By incorporating these strategies into everyday routines, parents can instill valuable life skills and foster a culture of preparedness within the family.

Special Considerations for Infants and Toddlers

Ensuring that emergency kits for infants and toddlers are well-stocked with essentials is paramount for meeting their unique needs during crises. These kits should include items such as diapers, formula, baby food, bottles, medications, and comfort items like blankets or stuffed animals. By proactively preparing for the specific needs of young children, parents can ensure their safety and well-being during emergencies.

Practicing evacuating with young children is essential for familiarizing them with evacuation procedures and ensuring a smooth process during actual emergencies. By using strollers, carriers, or car seats, parents can safely transport infants and toddlers while teaching older siblings how to assist in caring for younger ones. Further, by involving older siblings in the evacuation process, parents not only foster a sense of responsibility but also strengthen sibling bonds and teamwork skills.

Creating a communication plan with caregivers or family members who can assist with emergencies is vital, especially if parents are unavailable. This plan should outline important contact information, roles, and responsibilities, ensuring that everyone knows how to coordinate and communicate effectively during crises. By establishing clear lines of communication, parents can ensure that children receive the support and care they need, even in their absence.

Considerations for Older Children

For older children, teaching them how to call 911 or other emergency phone numbers in their area is an important skill that can empower them to take quick and appropriate action during emergencies. By understanding when it's appropriate to call for help, older children can play a proactive role in ensuring their safety and that of others around them.

Involving older children in creating a family emergency action plan is another valuable opportunity to teach them about preparedness and empower them to take responsibility for their safety. This plan should include designated meeting points, evacuation routes, and communication methods, ensuring that everyone knows what to do in different emergency scenarios.

Encouraging older children to undertake tasks suitable for their age helps strengthen their feelings of readiness and independence. Whether it's helping to pack emergency kits, leading younger siblings during drills, or memorizing important contact information, involving older children in preparedness activities fosters a sense of responsibility and confidence.

Providing opportunities for older children to learn basic first aid skills, such as CPR, choking rescue, and wound care, equips them with valuable life-saving knowledge. Through age-appropriate training programs or courses, parents can empower older children to respond effectively during medical emergencies and potentially save lives. By investing in their children's preparedness and safety, parents instill important life skills and confidence that will serve them well throughout their lives.

Childcare Emergency Action Plan

1. **Emergency Numbers:** Include the contact numbers of parents or legal guardians who can be reached in case of emergencies. List the phone numbers for local emergency services such as 911 or the equivalent emergency number in your area. Ensure you have the contact information for healthcare providers such as doctors, pediatricians, or specialists who may need to be contacted during emergencies.
2. **Evacuation Procedures:** Outline evacuation routes and meeting points in case of a fire, a natural disaster, or other emergencies.
3. **Medical Information:** Provide details about any medical conditions, allergies, medications, or special needs of your children.
4. **Communication Plan:** Specify how caregivers will communicate with parents during emergencies, such as through phone calls, text messages, or email updates.
5. **Emergency Supplies:** Ensure that the childcare facility is equipped with emergency supplies, including first aid kits, food, water, and essential medications.
6. **Staff Responsibilities:** Assign roles and responsibilities to childcare staff members, including who will lead

evacuations, administer first aid, and communicate with emergency responders.

7. **Regular Drills:** Conduct emergency drills regularly to practice evacuation procedures and ensure that both children and staff are prepared to respond effectively in emergencies.

By incorporating these tips and considerations into emergency plans, parents and caregivers can help children feel more confident, secure, and resilient in the face of unexpected events.

ELDERLY FAMILY MEMBERS' PREPAREDNESS

Preparing elderly family members for disasters and emergencies is paramount to safeguarding their safety and well-being. By taking proactive measures and crafting a comprehensive plan, caregivers can empower elderly individuals to navigate challenging situations more effectively.

Firstly, gather essential information to stay informed and prepared. Stay updated about potential hazards and evacuation procedures in your area by signing up for local emergency alerts and familiarizing yourself with community resources. Assess the specific needs and limitations of elderly family members, such as mobility issues, medical conditions, or dietary restrictions. Establish a robust support network comprising family members, neighbors, caregivers, and healthcare providers who can offer assistance during emergencies.

Next, take practical steps to develop a detailed emergency plan tailored to the needs of elderly family members. Create a comprehensive emergency plan outlining evacuation routes, emergency contacts, medical information, and any special accommodations required. Ensure that elderly family members have accessible emergency contacts and communication devices, such as cell phones or medical alert systems, to quickly seek assistance when needed.

Don't forget to gather basic emergency supplies like food, water, medications, flashlights, batteries, and a first aid kit. Manage medical and personal needs by ensuring an adequate supply of medications, medical supplies, and personal care items. Keep a record of medical information, including medications, allergies, and healthcare providers, in an easily accessible format.

Develop a detailed evacuation plan that includes transportation arrangements, shelter options, and provisions for pets or service animals. Plan for temperature control during emergencies by ensuring access to heating or cooling devices, blankets, and appropriate clothing. Additionally, ensure that elderly family members have updated legal documents, such as wills, powers of attorney, and advance directives, to facilitate decision-making during emergencies.

By proactively preparing elderly family members and addressing their specific needs, caregivers can enhance their resilience and ability to cope with disasters and emergencies effectively. It's essential to regularly review and update emergency plans and supplies to ensure readiness and adaptability to changing circumstances.

How to Recover After a Disaster

Recovering after a disaster can be a challenging process, but with the right approach, individuals can gradually restore their lives and properties. Let's look at some essential steps to take during the recovery phase.

Prioritize safety by waiting for authorities to declare it safe before returning home after a disaster. Before reentering the property, conduct a thorough inspection for damage and potential hazards. Be cautious of structural instability, gas leaks, electrical hazards, and other risks.

Seek guidance and support from reliable sources, such as local government agencies, community organizations, and reputable disaster relief organizations. These entities can provide valuable assistance, resources, and information to facilitate the recovery process. Stay informed about available services, assistance programs, and recovery efforts in your area.

Be sure to document property damage by capturing photographs or videos of the affected areas, then promptly reach out to your insurance providers to start the claims process and seek reimbursement for the damages. Provide detailed documentation, including descriptions of the damage, estimates for repair or replacement costs, and any relevant receipts or invoices. Take immediate steps to secure the property and prevent further damage, such as boarding up windows, covering roof openings, and removing debris.

By following these steps and collaborating with trusted sources, individuals can navigate the recovery process more effectively and work toward restoring their home and community in the aftermath of a disaster. Remember to prioritize safety, remain resilient, and seek support from others during this challenging time.

Checklist

Here's a checklist to ensure your safety and well-being:

1. Stay Informed

Stay updated about potential hazards and evacuation procedures in your area. Monitor weather alerts, news updates, and official announcements from local authorities.

2. Assess Specific Needs

Identify the specific needs and limitations of elderly family members and children, such as mobility issues, medical conditions, dietary restrictions, and medication requirements. Tailor your emergency plans and preparations accordingly.

3. Build a Support Network

Establish a reliable support network of caregivers, family members, neighbors, and healthcare providers who can assist during emergencies. Ensure that everyone understands their roles and responsibilities in the event of a crisis.

4. Create an Emergency Plan

Develop a detailed emergency plan that outlines evacuation routes, emergency contacts, medical information, and special accommodations for elderly family members. Review and update the plan regularly to account for any changes in circumstances or needs.

5. Stock Essential Supplies

Make sure to stock up on essential supplies and medications to last for an extended period. Ensure you have enough food, water, medications, medical supplies, personal hygiene items, and other necessities to cover your needs.

6. Keep Accessible Records

Maintain accessible records of medical information, including medications, allergies, medical conditions, and healthcare providers. Store copies of important documents such as identification, insurance policies, advance directives, and contact information for emergency services.

7. Develop an Evacuation Plan

Create a comprehensive evacuation plan that includes transportation arrangements, shelter options, and arrangements for pets or service animals. Practice evacuation drills with elderly family members to familiarize them with the process.

8. Prepare for Temperature Control

Plan for temperature control during emergencies by ensuring access to heating or cooling devices, blankets, and appropriate clothing. Consider the specific needs of elderly family members, especially those who may be more susceptible to extreme temperatures.

9. Seek Guidance and Manage Property Damage

Seek guidance from trusted sources, such as local government agencies, community organizations, and reputable disaster relief organizations. In the aftermath of a disaster, effectively manage property damage by documenting losses, contacting insurance providers, and taking steps to secure the property.

By following these steps and preparing before a disaster occurs, caregivers can help elderly family members stay safe, secure, and resilient during emergencies. Remember to communicate openly, address concerns, and prioritize safety at all times.

CONSIDERATIONS FOR PETS

Preparing your pets for disasters is essential to guarantee their safety and well-being during emergencies. As a pet owner, it falls on you to take proactive measures and devise a plan to safeguard your beloved furry companions.

Before a Disaster

First things first, create a detailed evacuation plan that includes your pets. Identify pet-friendly shelters, boarding facilities, or hotels in your area where you can take your pets if you need to evacuate. Plan your transportation routes accordingly, ensuring that your pets can safely accompany you.

Next, assemble an emergency kit tailored specifically for your pets. Be sure to include vital items such as food, water, medications, vaccination records, identification tags with your contact information, a leash or harness, a carrier or crate, bedding, litter, and a recent photo of your pet for identification purposes.

If you have large animals such as horses or livestock, it's important to ensure they have proper identification and access to shelter during emergencies. Additionally, stockpile enough food and water to last them through the duration of the emergency.

Stay informed about local emergency alerts, weather forecasts, and evacuation orders. Monitor official communication channels and follow the guidance provided by emergency management agencies. Act promptly to ensure the safety of both yourself and your pets during emergencies.

By being proactive and prepared, you can ensure that your pets are safe and well-cared for in the event of a disaster. Don't wait until it's too late—start planning and preparing today to protect your furry companions when they need it most.

During a Disaster

During a disaster, your pets' safety is just as important as yours. Let's look at what you need to do to ensure their well-being.

If You Evacuate

When evacuating, always take your pets with you. Remember, if it's not safe for you, it's not safe for them either. Make sure to bring their emergency kit, which should include essentials like food, water, medications, and comfort items. Secure them safely during transportation to prevent injuries.

If You Stay at Home

If you decide to stay home during a disaster, keep your pets indoors and bring them to your designated safe room if necessary. Monitor their behavior closely for signs of distress or anxiety, and provide comfort and reassurance as needed.

If You Must Evacuate Without Your Pets

In the unfortunate event that you must evacuate without your pets, confine them to a safe area inside the house with plenty of food, water, and bedding. Place a notice outside your home indicating that pets are inside and include contact numbers where you can be reached. This will help rescue teams locate and care for your pets until you can be reunited.

After a Disaster

After a disaster strikes, reuniting with your pets becomes a top priority. If you find yourself separated from your pets in the chaos of a disaster, focus first on ensuring your family's safety. Once everyone is secure, begin searching for your animals. Reach out to local shelters, veterinarians, and animal control agencies to report missing pets and enlist their help in locating them.

As you navigate the aftermath of a disaster, it's crucial to keep your pets secure. Avoid allowing them to roam loose outdoors, as hazards may still exist. Keep them on a leash or safely enclosed until it's deemed safe for them to roam freely.

If you encounter injured or stranded wild animals in the aftermath of a disaster, don't hesitate to seek assistance. Contact your local emergency management office or animal control agency to report the situation and provide aid to the animals in need.

Understand that disasters can be just as traumatic for animals as they are for humans. Your pets may exhibit changes in behavior or require extra care and attention during this time. Be patient, offer comfort and reassurance, and provide the necessary care they need to recover from the ordeal.

By following these guidelines and preparing in advance, you can ensure the safety and well-being of your beloved pets during emergencies. Remember, proactive planning and quick action are essential for protecting your pets and minimizing risks in the aftermath of a disaster.

Taking care of our loved ones—both human and animal—is a sacred duty that reflects the depth of our compassion and responsibility. As it's written in 1 Timothy 5:8: "But if any provide not for his own, and especially for those of his own house, he hath denied the faith, and is worse than an infidel" (*King James Bible*, 2020). This verse reminds us of the importance of caring for all members of our family, ensuring their safety, well-being, and security in times of need. Let us strive to fulfill this duty with love, diligence, and unwavering commitment, knowing that our actions speak volumes about our faith and character.

BUILDING A SUPPORTIVE COMMUNITY

I n times of crisis, the support of a strong and united community can make all the difference. As we embark on the journey of building a supportive community for emergency preparedness, let us reflect on the wisdom found in Hebrews 10:24-25: "And let us consider one another to provoke unto love and to good works: Not forsaking the assembling of ourselves together, as the manner of some is; but exhorting one another: and so much the more, as ye see the day approaching" (*King James Bible*, 2024b).

This chapter serves as a guide to help us establish and fortify relationships within our local church and community, recognizing the significance of communal support during times of crisis. As we move forward in emergency preparedness, let us remember the words of Hebrews 10:24-25 and continue to provoke one another unto love and good works, strengthening our bonds of fellowship and mutual support as we face the challenges that might lie ahead.

BUILDING RELATIONSHIPS WITH NEIGHBORS AND OUR COMMUNITY

In times of need, the support of neighbors and the broader community can be invaluable. Establishing connections and fostering relationships within our neighborhood not only enhances our sense of belonging but also creates a network of support that can be crucial during emergencies.

Firstly, knowing our neighbors and building a network of support is vital for several reasons. It fosters a sense of community and unity where neighbors look out for one another. In times of crisis, having familiar faces to turn to for assistance or guidance can provide comfort and reassurance. Additionally, neighbors can offer practical help, such as sharing resources, providing shelter, or assisting with evacuation plans. By building strong relationships with our neighbors, we create a support system that enhances our collective resilience and ability to respond effectively to emergencies.

Organizing community initiatives to strengthen relationships and preparedness is a proactive step toward building a resilient neighborhood. Here are some key steps to consider:

1. Decide which families to include. Identify households within the neighborhood that are interested in participating in community-building activities and emergency preparedness efforts.
2. Choose a meeting date. Select a convenient date and time for the initial neighborhood gathering. Consider factors such as work schedules and family commitments to maximize attendance.
3. Collect contact information. Gather contact information from participating households, including phone numbers,

email addresses, and physical addresses. This ensures effective communication and coordination in emergencies.

4. Get to know each other. Use the initial meeting as an opportunity for neighbors to introduce themselves and share basic information about their families. Encourage open dialogue and foster a sense of camaraderie among participants.

5. Consider a skill/resources meeting. Organize a follow-up meeting where neighbors can share their skills, expertise, and resources. This could include individuals with medical training, handyman skills, or access to emergency supplies.

6. Hold an emergency kit meeting. Host a meeting dedicated to discussing and assembling emergency kits for households within the neighborhood. Guide essential items to include and offer assistance to those who may need help preparing their kits.

7. Research and gather additional information. Continuously seek out resources and information relevant to emergency preparedness in your area. Stay informed about local hazards, evacuation routes, emergency shelters, and community resources available during disasters.

In addition to these organizational steps, it's essential to compile a list of resources available within the community. This could include contact information for local emergency services, medical facilities, community centers, volunteer organizations, and neighborhood watch groups. By having access to these resources, neighbors can quickly mobilize support and assistance when needed, further strengthening the community's resilience in the face of adversity.

By prioritizing relationships with neighbors and taking proactive steps to organize and prepare together, we can build a resilient and supportive community that stands ready to face any challenges that may arise.

The Role of the Church in Community Support and Preparedness

The church plays a unique and crucial role in providing support and assistance to its members and the broader community during times of crisis. As a spiritual and social hub, the church community offers a supportive network that can help individuals reacclimate, recover, and reassure one another in the aftermath of disasters.

Firstly, the church serves as a place of reacclimation for individuals who may have been displaced or affected by a crisis. In the immediate aftermath of a disaster, congregants can find solace and support within the familiar walls of their church. Whether that entails providing shelter, distributing essential supplies, or offering emotional support, the church community can help individuals feel grounded and connected during times of uncertainty.

Secondly, the church plays a vital role in facilitating recovery efforts within the community. Through outreach programs, volunteer initiatives, and fundraising efforts, congregants can come together to provide practical assistance to those in need. Whether it's rebuilding homes, organizing food drives, or offering counseling services, the collective strength of the church community can significantly aid in the recovery process.

Lastly, the church serves as a source of reassurance and hope during challenging times. Through prayer, spiritual guidance, and pastoral care, church leaders can offer comfort and encouragement to individuals grappling with loss, trauma, or uncertainty. The sense of faith and fellowship that permeates the church community can provide a beacon of hope amid the darkness of disaster, helping individuals find strength and resilience in their faith.

Through regular attendance, volunteering, and participation in church events, individuals can cultivate meaningful connections with fellow congregants, creating a sense of belonging and solidarity that transcends individual crises.

In times of need, the church community stands ready to offer support, assistance, and comfort to its members and the wider community. Individuals can tap into a rich source of support and resilience that can help them navigate the challenges of emergencies with strength and grace.

CREATING OR JOINING A PREPAREDNESS GROUP

Organizing or joining a community preparedness group is a proactive step toward enhancing your ability to navigate emergencies and disasters effectively. These groups play a vital role in fostering cooperation, sharing knowledge, and providing support during challenging times. Here's a closer look at the functions of a community preparedness group:

1. **Collaboration:** One of the primary functions of a community preparedness group is to facilitate cooperation and collaboration among its members. By pooling resources, knowledge, and skills, the group can effectively address various challenges and mitigate risks during emergencies.
2. **Education:** Community preparedness groups provide valuable education and training on emergency preparedness, survival skills, and self-sufficiency. These educational initiatives empower members with the knowledge and tools they need to respond effectively to different types of emergencies.
3. **Support:** During crises, community preparedness groups provide essential emotional support, encouragement, and assistance to their members. This support network plays a vital role in helping individuals cope with stress, anxiety, and uncertainty, ultimately fostering resilience and aiding in the community's recovery process.
4. **Planning:** A key function of community preparedness groups is to develop comprehensive emergency plans, evacuation procedures, and communication strategies. By proactively planning and preparing for various scenarios, the group can minimize the impact of emergencies and ensure a coordinated response.

5. **Networking:** Community preparedness groups establish connections with local authorities, emergency services, and other community organizations. These networks enhance communication, coordination, and resource-sharing during emergencies, strengthening the community's overall resilience.

Overall, community preparedness groups play a vital role in building resilient communities and empowering individuals to effectively respond to emergencies and disasters. By organizing or joining such a group, you can contribute to creating a safer and more prepared community for yourself and others.

Joining a Preparedness Group

Joining a preparedness group can be a wise decision, but it's crucial to assess several factors before committing. If you're contemplating joining a preparedness group, several key factors warrant consideration. Firstly, strong leadership within the group is paramount. Look for groups led by individuals who demonstrate dedication, capability, and adeptness in organizing and coordinating group activities. Effective leadership ensures that the group operates efficiently and effectively in pursuit of its preparedness goals.

Additionally, seek out groups whose members share similar values, goals, and levels of commitment to preparedness efforts. Like-mindedness among members fosters cohesion and facilitates collaboration toward common objectives. It ensures that everyone within the group is aligned in their approach and dedicated to preparing for emergencies.

Furthermore, organization within the group is essential for its functionality. Opt for groups with clear objectives, structured meetings, and effective communication channels. A well-organized group ensures that tasks are delegated efficiently, meetings are productive, and information is disseminated promptly, facilitating smooth coordination and collaboration among members.

Lastly, focus on the groups that prioritize security and safety measures. Look for groups that implement safety protocols, maintain confidentiality, and cultivate trust among members. A secure and supportive environment is crucial for fostering a sense of safety and confidence within the group, enabling members to engage fully in preparedness activities without concerns for their well-being.

Creating a Preparedness Group

Creating a preparedness group is a proactive step toward enhancing community resilience and readiness in the face of emergencies or disasters. Here's a comprehensive guide on how to organize an effective community preparedness group:

Steps to Organize

Identify Interested Members

Reach out to neighbors, friends, and community members who share an interest in preparedness. Utilize social media, community forums, or local gatherings to connect with potential members.

Define Group Goals

Clarify the purpose and objectives of the group. Determine whether the focus will be on mutual aid, skill-sharing, resource-sharing, or a combination of these. Establish clear goals to guide the group's activities.

Establish Leadership

Select individuals with strong leadership skills and a commitment to the group's mission to serve as organizers or coordinators. Leadership should be inclusive, collaborative, and capable of effectively managing group dynamics.

Set Meeting Schedule

Determine a regular meeting schedule that accommodates the availability of members. Consider factors such as work schedules, family commitments, and other obligations when setting meeting times. Consistency is key to maintaining momentum and engagement.

Create Communication Channels

Establish communication channels, such as email lists, social media groups, or messaging apps, to facilitate information sharing and coordination among members. Ensure that all members have access to these channels and are encouraged to participate actively.

Develop an Action Plan

Outline specific tasks, responsibilities, and goals for the group to accomplish. This may include conducting training sessions, organizing drills, developing emergency kits, or coordinating community outreach efforts. Assign roles and delegate responsibilities accordingly.

Hold Regular Meetings

To maintain effective communication and coordination, it's important to conduct regular meetings within the community preparedness group. These meetings should be used to discuss progress, address concerns, and plan future activities. Developing agendas for each meeting ensures that discussions remain focused and productive. Additionally, encourage active participation from all members and provide opportunities for feedback and input to foster collaboration and inclusivity within the group.

Create an Agenda

- Develop a plan for each meeting to ensure that discussions remain focused and productive. Clearly outline topics to be covered and allocate time for each agenda item.

Encourage Participation

- Create a welcoming and inclusive environment that encourages all members to contribute ideas and suggestions. Foster open communication and constructive dialogue among members.

Rotate Leadership

- Rotate meeting facilitators or chairs to distribute leadership responsibilities and foster a sense of ownership among members. This promotes inclusivity and ensures that different perspectives are represented.

Provide Training

- Offer training sessions on relevant topics, such as first aid, communication skills, or emergency response procedures. Encourage members to share their expertise and experiences with the group.

Foster Camaraderie

- Organize social events or activities outside of meetings to build camaraderie and strengthen relationships among members. This enhances cohesion and promotes a sense of community within the group.

What should you do when asked to give a presentation?

1. Prepare content. Develop informative and engaging presentations on topics related to emergency preparedness, survival skills, or community resilience. Tailor the content to the audience's interests and needs.
2. Tailor to the audience. Customize your presentation to address the specific needs and interests of the audience. Consider factors such as demographics, prior knowledge, and level of engagement when designing the presentation.
3. Encourage interaction. Include interactive elements, such as Q&A sessions, group discussions, or hands-on demonstrations, to engage the audience and encourage participation. Foster an interactive and engaging learning environment.
4. Provide resources. Offer handouts, guides, or online resources to supplement the presentation and provide additional information for attendees. Ensure that attendees have access to resources that can help them further explore the topic.

By following these steps and guidelines, you can organize an effective community preparedness group that empowers members to collaborate, learn, and take proactive steps toward enhancing community resilience and readiness.

Remember, whether you're organizing or joining a preparedness group, the strength found in the community can empower individuals to achieve great things together. As Mother Teresa once said, "I can do things you cannot, you can do things I cannot; together we can do great things" ("A Quote by Mother Teresa," 2023). By working together and supporting one another, we can better prepare for and respond to emergencies, creating safer and more resilient communities.

MAINTAINING YOUR PREPAREDNESS PLAN

"Excellence is not an act but a habit," wrote Will Durant ("Quotes From Will Durant", n.d), underscoring the importance of consistent effort and vigilance in achieving success. This sentiment rings especially true in the realm of emergency preparedness where ongoing commitment and regular practice are key to ensuring the safety and well-being of ourselves and our loved ones.

Preparedness is not a one-time task; it's an ongoing process that requires regular attention and effort. Just as we engage in daily habits to maintain our physical and mental well-being, so too must we cultivate habits of preparedness to safeguard against unforeseen emergencies.

Set aside time at regular intervals to review and update your preparedness plans. Circumstances change, and so should your plans. Whether it's changes in family dynamics, living arrangements, or community resources, staying informed and adjusting your plans accordingly is essential.

Regularly practice emergency drills with your family to ensure everyone knows their roles and responsibilities. Conduct fire drills, evacuation exercises, and emergency scenarios to reinforce preparedness skills and reduce panic in real-life situations.

Keep abreast of current events, local hazards, and emerging threats that may impact your area. Subscribe to emergency alerts, participate in community preparedness events, and stay connected with local authorities to stay informed and prepared.

Preparedness is a team effort that requires the involvement of every family member. Encourage open communication, delegate tasks, and involve children in age-appropriate preparedness activities to foster a culture of readiness within your household.

Aim for ongoing enhancement in your preparedness endeavors. Take lessons from previous encounters, gather input from family members, and integrate these insights into your plans. Keep in mind that preparedness is a continuous journey not a fixed endpoint, and there's constantly space for refinement.

By incorporating these habits of preparedness into your daily routine, you can cultivate a culture of safety and resilience within your family. Just as excellence is achieved through consistent effort and practice, so too is effective emergency preparedness.

REGULAR UPDATES TO YOUR PREPAREDNESS PLAN

Ensuring that your emergency plan remains relevant and effective requires regular review and updates to accommodate changes in family dynamics, living situations, or local risks. Family members should actively participate in reviewing their responsibilities and procedures every six months to ensure everyone is familiar with the plan as well as any adjustments that may have been made.

The necessity of these regular updates cannot be overstated as circumstances may change over time, requiring adaptations to your preparedness strategy. Whether it's the addition of new family members, changes in living arrangements, or shifts in local hazards, staying proactive and flexible in your approach to emergency planning is crucial for maintaining readiness.

To assist with this process, consider utilizing resources such as the Family Emergency Plan provided by the Office of Disaster Preparedness and Management (ODPM) or the Family Emergency Communication Planning Document offered by Ready.gov. These resources offer comprehensive templates and guidelines for assessing and updating your emergency plans, ensuring they remain current and effective.

Let's take a look at a step-by-step guide to assess and update emergency kits and plans.

1. Review Your Family Disaster Plan

Gather Family Members

Gather all household members to review the specifics of your current emergency plan, which should involve discussing evacuation routes, designated meeting spots, and communication procedures.

Update Contact Information

Verify and update contact information for family members, emergency contacts, and essential services. Ensure that everyone has access to updated phone numbers, addresses, and email addresses.

Evaluate Meeting Locations

Assess the suitability of designated meeting locations in case of separation during an emergency. Consider factors such as accessibility, safety, and proximity to home or work.

Discuss Changes

Encourage open communication to discuss any changes or updates needed to the family disaster plan. Address concerns and incorporate feedback from all family members to ensure the plan is comprehensive and practical.

2. Check Your Disaster Supplies Kit

Inventory Check

Perform a comprehensive inventory of your disaster supplies kit to evaluate its contents. This encompasses assessing food, water, medications, first aid supplies, tools, and other vital items.

Check Expiration Dates

Pay close attention to expiration dates on stored food, water, and medications. Discard any items that have expired, and replace them with fresh supplies to maintain effectiveness during an emergency.

Inspect Equipment

Inspect equipment such as flashlights, batteries, portable radios, and emergency tools to ensure they are in working condition. Replace or repair any damaged or malfunctioning items.

Consider Special Needs

Take into account any special needs or requirements of family members, such as infants, elderly individuals, or individuals with medical conditions. Customize your disaster supplies kit accordingly to meet these needs.

3. Update Contact Information

Compile a Contact List

Create a comprehensive contact list that includes emergency contacts, family members, neighbors, local authorities, and utility companies. Keep multiple copies of this list in an accessible location, such as in your disaster supplies kit and on your smartphone.

Communicate Changes

Communicate any changes to contact information with family members and designated emergency contacts. Ensure that everyone knows who to contact in case of an emergency and how to reach them.

4. Rehearse Emergency Scenarios

Conduct Practice Drills

Organize practice drills to simulate various emergency scenarios, such as fires, earthquakes, or severe weather events. Practice evacuating your home; use emergency supplies and ensure proper communication with family members throughout the drill.

Identify Weak Points

Evaluate your family's response to each scenario and identify any areas that may need improvement. This may include refining evacuation routes, practicing emergency communication protocols, or updating emergency procedures.

Assign Roles

Assign specific roles and responsibilities to each family member during an emergency. Ensure that everyone understands their role and knows how to fulfill it effectively.

By following this step-by-step guide, you can assess and update your emergency kits and plans effectively, ensuring that your family is prepared to respond to any emergency confidently and efficiently. Regular review and maintenance of emergency preparedness measures are essential to staying resilient and ready for the unexpected.

By regularly reviewing and updating your preparedness plan and emergency kits, you can better adapt to changing circumstances and maintain readiness for whatever challenges may arise. Remember, preparedness is a continuous process, and staying proactive is key to ensuring the safety and well-being of your family.

PRACTICING YOUR PREPAREDNESS PLAN

Family emergency drills are crucial practice sessions designed to help family members prepare for emergencies by simulating various scenarios and practicing appropriate responses. These drills offer an opportunity for everyone to familiarize themselves with emergency procedures, roles, and responsibilities, ensuring a coordinated and effective response when faced with a real crisis.

The importance of these drills cannot be overstated as they help build confidence, reduce anxiety, and enhance readiness for unexpected situations.

Before conducting family emergency drills, it's essential to make necessary preparations to ensure a smooth and effective practice session. This includes discussing the purpose and goals of the drill with family members, setting clear expectations, and explaining the importance of active participation. Consider utilizing resources such as preparedness drills for kids, which offer step-by-step instructions and age-appropriate activities for different emergency scenarios.

Here are some common preparedness drills to do with the whole family:

1. **House fire:** Practice evacuation procedures, identify escape routes, locate smoke alarms, and discuss how to use a fire extinguisher.
2. **Tornado, earthquake, or other natural disaster:** Review safety protocols for sheltering in place or evacuating to a safe location during severe weather events.
3. **Stranger danger:** Role-play scenarios to teach your children how to recognize and respond to potentially dangerous situations with strangers.
4. **Car accident:** Demonstrate how to safely exit a vehicle and seek help in the event of a car accident.
5. **Active shooter:** Discuss strategies for sheltering in place, escaping, or engaging with law enforcement during an active shooter situation.
6. **Home invaders:** Practice the appropriate responses, procedures, lockdown procedures, and emergency communication methods to alert authorities.

7. **CPR and first aid:** Review basic first aid techniques, and practice cardiopulmonary resuscitation (CPR) on training mannequins.
8. **Social preparedness:** Discuss how to communicate and coordinate with neighbors, friends, and community members during emergencies.

To integrate these practices into your family's routine, contemplate scheduling regular drills and setting calendar reminders to maintain consistency. Stress the significance of participation, and foster open communication to tackle any questions or concerns that may arise during drills.

Additionally, family camping and hiking trips can serve as enjoyable and practical opportunities to practice "bugging out" and apply preparedness skills in a real-world setting. These outings provide valuable hands-on experience in navigation, shelter building, food preparation, and survival techniques, fostering resilience and self-reliance in family members. By incorporating preparedness activities into fun recreational activities like camping, families can enhance their readiness and bond through shared experiences in the great outdoors.

PREPAREDNESS AS AN ONGOING JOURNEY

Preparedness is not a destination but rather an ongoing journey that requires continual attention and dedication. It's about understanding that the world is ever-changing, and being prepared means adapting to those changes to keep yourself and your loved ones safe.

Integrating preparedness activities into your daily routine is essential for maintaining readiness and ensuring that you are well-equipped to handle emergencies when they arise. These activities don't have to be elaborate or time-consuming; even simple tasks can make a significant difference in your level of preparedness.

Regularly checking your emergency supplies is a fundamental preparedness activity. This ensures that your supplies are up-to-date, well-maintained, and readily accessible when needed. By incorporating this task into your routine, such as conducting a quick inventory check every month or so, you can identify any missing or expired items and replenish them promptly.

Reviewing evacuation plans is another crucial aspect of preparedness. Knowing what to do and where to go in the event of an emergency can save valuable time and potentially lives. Take time to regularly review your evacuation routes and meeting points with your family, ensuring that everyone is familiar with the plan and knows what to do in different scenarios.

Practicing basic first aid skills is also essential for preparedness. Accidents and injuries can happen anytime and anywhere, so having the knowledge and confidence to administer basic first aid can make a significant difference in an emergency. Incorporating regular first aid practice sessions into your routine, whether through online tutorials or hands-on training courses, ensures that you are well-prepared to provide immediate assistance when needed.

Additionally, staying informed about potential hazards, local emergency procedures, and community alerts is crucial for effective preparedness. By keeping up-to-date with news updates, weather forecasts, and community alerts through various channels such as television, radio, social media, and emergency notification apps, you can stay informed about potential risks and take proactive measures to mitigate them.

Overall, integrating preparedness activities into your daily life ensures that preparedness becomes a natural part of your lifestyle rather than an occasional chore. By consistently checking emergency supplies, reviewing evacuation plans, practicing first aid skills, and staying informed about potential hazards, you can maintain a high level of readiness and better protect yourself and your family in the event of an emergency.

By making preparedness a habit, you cultivate a mindset of readiness and resilience that permeates every aspect of your life. Consistent effort and vigilance not only enhance your ability to respond effectively to emergencies but also reduce your vulnerabilities in the face of unexpected challenges. Keep in mind that preparedness is not a single event but an ongoing journey that demands constant dedication and diligence to safeguard the safety and well-being of both you and your loved ones.

In conclusion, the journey of preparedness is not a sprint but a marathon, requiring persistence and continuous improvement to ensure our readiness for whatever challenges may come our way. As the scripture from Galatians 6:9 wisely counsels, "And let us not be weary in well doing: for in due season we shall reap if we faint not" (*King James Bible*, 2018).

It's crucial to recognize that preparedness is not a destination but a continuous process, requiring ongoing dedication and commitment. By remaining steadfast in our resolve to be prepared, we can better safeguard ourselves, our families, and our communities against the uncertainties of the future.

Embracing preparedness as an ongoing journey means constantly striving to improve our readiness, whether through refining our emergency plans, updating our supplies, or enhancing our skills. Each small step we take toward preparedness contributes to a safer and more resilient future for all.

Inspire Someone Else to Prepare!

You have all the knowledge you need to prepare your family for the unexpected – and that makes you the best person to inspire someone else to do the same thing.

Simply by sharing your honest opinion of this book and a little about your own preparedness journey, you'll inspire new readers to equip themselves with all the knowledge they need to protect their families.

LET'S HEAR WHAT YOU THINK!

Thank you so much for your support. You can face any challenge that comes your way, and your words will help someone else to do the same.

Leave a Review

CONCLUSION

In today's volatile world, achieving peace of mind amid uncertainties is crucial, and preparedness holds the solution. Throughout this book, we've explored the vital role of readiness in handling emergencies. It's not a one-time task but a continuous process of proactive actions. By evaluating risks, crafting emergency plans, and conducting drills, you empower yourself and your family to effectively navigate unforeseen challenges.

Remember, family preparedness doesn't have to be complicated or expensive. By implementing straightforward strategies tailored to your household's needs, you can effectively safeguard your loved ones in times of uncertainty.

In times of crisis, establishing effective communication channels is crucial for families to stay connected and informed. This entails devising a clear communication plan outlining how family members will reach each other during emergencies. It's imperative to include contact information for local authorities, emergency services, and out-of-town relatives in this plan. Additionally, designating a predetermined meeting place in case family members are separated and unable to return home ensures a coordinated response amid chaos.

Ensuring access to basic emergency supplies is paramount for family preparedness, so assembling a comprehensive emergency kit comprising non-perishable food, water, medications, first aid supplies, flashlights, batteries, and a multi-tool is essential. Storing these supplies in a designated location that is easily accessible to all family members facilitates quick access during crises, enhancing overall preparedness and resilience.

Implementing home safety measures is essential for reducing risks during emergencies. Installing smoke detectors, carbon monoxide detectors, and fire extinguishers improves early detection and response to potential hazards. Securing heavy furniture and appliances helps prevent them from toppling during earthquakes or other disasters, thus minimizing injuries and property damage. Additionally, becoming familiar with utility shut-off procedures for gas, water, and electricity further enhances home safety and preparedness.

Financial preparedness plays a critical role in weathering unforeseen emergencies. Setting aside an emergency fund to cover unexpected expenses ensures financial stability during crises. Aim to save at least three to six months' worth of living expenses in a savings account or emergency fund to cushion against financial shocks. Additionally, considering adequate insurance coverage for home, health, and belongings mitigates financial risks and provides peace of mind during challenging times.

Regular emergency drills are essential for ensuring family members know how to respond effectively during various scenarios. Conducting fire drills, earthquake drills, and evacuation drills regularly reinforces safety procedures and minimizes panic during real emergencies. Familiarizing oneself with community resources and emergency services available in the area, including nearby shelters, hospitals, and evacuation routes, further enhances preparedness. Further, staying informed about local hazards and emergency alerts issued by authorities enables proactive responses to potential threats, fostering a culture of resilience within the community.

May this journey toward preparedness serve as a beacon of hope and resilience, assuring us that even in life's trials, there is divine protection. Let us fortify our families with emergency plans guided by the spirit of resilience inspired by these words, instilling the confidence to face any challenge that may arise.

As we embark on the path of preparedness, let us heed the call to action: Embrace preparedness as a way of life, starting today. Step by step, let us build a future where we and our loved ones are ready for whatever lies ahead. Your feedback is invaluable. If you found this book beneficial, please consider leaving a review to empower more individuals to embrace preparedness and cultivate resilient communities. Together, let us journey forward with courage, wisdom, and preparedness.

ACKNOWLEDGMENTS

I would like to take a moment to acknowledge and thank those who have influenced and supported me in so many ways. To my Mom, who is missed every day, and Dad for all the love, support, and encouragement you both have given me over the years. I know I didn't make it easy on you. Dad, you have and continue to always set the example for me to be a better man. My stepmother, "Mama Hawk," for being a second mother to me and a wonderful grandmother to my son, you will be missed. My son, Carl, you amaze me with the man you are becoming, and I am blessed that the Lord allowed me to be your Dad. You have taught me patience and perseverance, and I am proud of you more than you will ever know. I love you more than you could imagine. My little sister, Tammi, who though you are shorter than me, you are head and shoulders above me with your never-ending love, encouragement, support, and straightforwardness. I love our talks! My brother-in-law, David, for being the man you are. You're a great husband and father, and I have the utmost respect for you ever since we first met. My two stepbrothers, John and Chris, y'all continue to be a lot of fun to be around, especially water skiing on the lake at night! Y'all are married to two wonderful, loving, and supportive women I am proud to call my sisters (in-laws). My grandmother, Gram, was the strongest and most loving woman I know, who loved life and always had fun! I will miss our talks and those amazing tea cakes! Aunt Jackie and Cousin Bonnie, y'all are two of the strongest and flat-out straightforward women I have ever known, and you do what it takes to get things done. Don't ever change! Uncle Mike, I have admired you; growing up, I always wanted to be like you. You have been and continue to be a great influence on me, and over the years, all the advice you gave did not fall on deaf ears. Aunt Robin, you are one amazing woman for putting up with Uncle Mike all these years!

I want to thank everyone who has been and currently is in my Sunday School class. Y'all have supported my son and me incredibly over the years, and I am deeply grateful. Y'all have always stepped up in times of personal crisis, and for that, I truly love you. Also, to my church family who have been such a loving and supportive group of people I enjoy seeing weekly. I wish I could name everyone, but seeing as I would most likely forget someone, I will say thank you all.

To my Sista & Braddah, Kuulei & Pale. Thank you for all your Aloha all these years, from Nanakuli to South Dakota! We love you guys (and Hoku)! To Don and Marie of BEAR Safety & Security Solutions, LLC. I never expected a firearm training class I found online would turn into a wonderful friendship. You two are awesome and an inspiration to me.

I appreciate my co-workers at the WW who are some of the best and most supportive people I know. I am blessed to work with y'all, and I count many of you as good friends.

A special thank you to my Lord and Savior, Jesus Christ, for His unfathomable grace and mercy in my life.

AUTHOR BIO

Scott C. Pyron is a resilient and devoted single father of a teenage son, deeply rooted in his Christian conservative and patriotic values. His life journey is a remarkable tapestry of professional achievement and personal dedication. For over 30 years, Scott has been a dynamic presence in the Information Technology industry, with a career that spans several countries around the world, giving him a broad perspective on global and local challenges. His transition to homesteading nearly a decade ago represents a significant and meaningful shift in his life. Settling on a quaint homestead in a small town in Alabama, Scott lives a life that echoes his beliefs in self-reliance and sustainable living. Scott's deep-rooted passion for helping others is evident in his dedication to sharing with individuals and families about crisis preparedness. Drawing from his extensive IT background and his practical experience in homesteading, he offers a unique and valuable perspective on preparing for emergencies. His approach to family preparedness is infused with his Christian faith and patriotic spirit, emphasizing the importance of community, self-sufficiency, and proactive planning. Living with his son and their chickens on their Alabama homestead, Scott C. Pyron continues to be a guiding light for those seeking to navigate the complexities of modern life with the wisdom and simplicity of traditional values. His work stands as a beacon for anyone looking to build a secure, prepared, and meaningful life amidst an ever-changing world.

REFERENCES

Adleman, R. (2023, July 19). *Antibiotics*. Patient.info. https://patient.info/infections/antibiotics-leaflet

Anderson, L. A. (2011, November 22). *Antibiotics guide*. Drugs. https://www.drugs.com/article/antibiotics.html

Andress, E., Ph.D., & Harrison, J., Ph.D. (2016). *Preparing an emergency food supply, and short-term food storage*. College of Family and Consumer Sciences University of Georgia. https://www.fcs.uga.edu/extension/preparing-an-emergency-food-supply-short-term-food-storage

Bedford, L. (2023a, March 26). *8 emergency preparedness drills for your kids - survival mom*. The Survival Mom. https://thesurvivalmom.com/try-it-today-preparedness-drills-kids/

Bedford, L. (2023b, August 23). *How to organize a community preparedness group & run it well - the survival mom*. The Survival Mom. https://thesurvivalmom.com/get-family-friends-board-prepping/

Before, during, and after a flood, (2024). Susquehanna Flood Forecasting. https://www.susquehannafloodforecasting.org/before-during-after.html

Benisek, A. (2021, November 5). *Antivirals for COVID-19: What you need to know*. WebMD. https://www.webmd.com/covid/antivirals-covid-19

Benjamin Franklin Quotes. (n.d.). *By failing to prepare, you are preparing to fail*. BrainyQuote. https://www.brainyquote.com/quotes/benjamin_franklin_138217

Bradford, A. (2024, January 26). *Guide to proper home security maintenance*. Safe Wise. https://www.safewise.com/security-system-maintenance-checklist/

Brennan, D.. (2021, October 4). *What are the top 10 most prescribed drugs?* MedicineNet. https://www.medicinenet.com/what_are_the_top_10_most_prescribed_drugs/article.htm

Brouhard, R. (2023). *Basic first aid you should know*. Verywell Health. https://www.verywellhealth.com/basic-first-aid-procedures-1298578

Brown, J. (2015, April 24). *Churches play a growing role in emergency management*. GovTech. https://www.govtech.com/em/disaster/churches-playing-growing-role-emergency-management.html

Brown, J. J. (2016, September 28). *National preparedness month: Home safety and security tips*. Nrablog. https://www.nrablog.com/articles/2016/9/national-preparedness-month-home-safety-and-security-tips

Build a kit. (2023). Ready.gov. https://www.ready.gov/kit

Cherry, K.. (2022, October 6). *Use these 10 tips to improve your resilience.* Verywell Mind. https://www.verywellmind.com/ways-to-become-more-resilient-2795063

Children in disasters real stories: Kevin's story. (2020, February 20). Centers for Disease Control and Prevention. https://www.cdc.gov/childrenindisasters/real-stories/emergencyplanning/kevin.html

Compendium of sanitation technologies in emergencies. (2016). Emergency-Wash. https://www.emergency-wash.org/water/en/technologies/technology/safe-water-storage

Corliss, J. (2020, October). *Staying positive during difficult times.* Harvard Health. https://www.health.harvard.edu/blog/staying-positive-during-difficult-times-2020100121047

Courier, F. C. (2010, October 22). *The importance of family emergency preparedness.* U.S. Army. https://www.army.mil/article/47058/the_importance_of_family_emergency_preparedness

Cunha, J. P. (2021a, July 9). *Omeprazole: Side effects, uses, dosage, interactions, warnings.* RxList. https://www.rxlist.com/omeprazole/generic-drug.htm

Cunha, J. P. (2021b, August 5). *Naproxen: Side effects, uses, dosage, interactions, warnings.* RxList. https://www.rxlist.com/naproxen/generic-drug.htm

Dale. (2013, November 3). *10 home security measures you should take now before SHTF.* Survivalist Prepper. https://survivalistprepper.net/10-home-security-measures-take-now/

Davis, C. P. (2021, March 29). *Medical definition of aspirin.* RxList. https://www.rxlist.com/aspirin/definition.htm

Davis, P. (2011, November 1). *7 strategies for building your family's resilience.* Psychology Today. https://www.psychologytoday.com/intl/blog/pressure-proof/201111/7-strategies-building-your-familys-resilience

Family communications plan. (2024). Habitat for Humanity. https://www.habitat.org/our-work/disaster-response/disaster-preparedness-homeowners/family-communications-plan

Family evacuation plan. (2024). Habitat for Humanity. https://www.habitat.org/our-work/disaster-response/disaster-preparedness-homeowners/family-evacuation-plan

Family preparedness plan. (2024). Habitat for Humanity. https://www.habitat.org/our-work/disaster-response/disaster-preparedness-homeowners/family-preparedness-plan

Floods and flash floods. (2024). Habitat for Humanity. https://www.habitat.org/our-work/disaster-response/disaster-preparedness-homeowners/floods

Earthquake preparedness: What to do before, during, and after. (2024). Quakekare.

https://www.quakekare.com/earthquake-preparedness

8 steps to building a complete 72-hour emergency kit. (2021). Family Survival Planning. https://www.familysurvivalplanning.com/72-hour-kit.html

Emergency kits. (2021). Wa.gov.au. https://www.dfes.wa.gov.au/hazard-informa tion/emergency-kits#:

Family disaster plan. (2024). Disaster center. https://disastercenter.com/New% 20Guide/Family%20Disaster%20Plan.html#:

Family emergency drill: How to prepare. (2023, April 24). Total Prepare. https://total prepare.ca/family-emergency-drill-how-to-prepare/

Farney, B. (2022, November 21). *12 must-know security tips for apartments*. Forbes. https://www.forbes.com/home-improvement/home-security/security-tips- for-apartments/

Floods: Before, during, and after. (2024). Red Cross Canada. https://www.redcross. ca/how-we-help/emergencies-and-disasters-in-canada/types-of-emergencies/ floods

Food preservation: The best ways to store food for an emergency. (2020, August 18). Homestead or Dead. https://www.homesteadordead.com/blog/food-preserva tion-the-best-ways-to-store-food-for-an-emergency

Freitag, T. (2023, October 24). *Emergency funds: Importance, benefits, and how to build one - Cleveland State Bank*. Cleveland State Bank. https://clevelandstate.bank/ emergency-funds-importance-benefits-and-how-to-build-one/

Graziosi, Dean. *50 PREPARATION QUOTES TO GET YOU STARTED ON THE RIGHT TRACK*. LinkedIn. Last modified April 5, 2022. https://www.linkedin. com/pulse/50-preparation-quotes-get-you-started-right-track-dean-graziosi/

Gun owner safety training. (2020). Everytown. https://www.everytown.org/solu tions/safety-training/

Home emergency preparedness plans for children - arrowhead. (2023, October 3). Arrowhead Communications. https://www.arrowheadgrp.com/blog/home- emergency-preparedness-plan-for-children/

How to can: A beginner's guide to canning food. (2023). Ball Mason Jars. https://www. ballmasonjars.com/canning-and-preserving-101.html

How to prepare before a disaster occurs. (2024). Redcross.org. https://www.redcross. org/get-help/how-to-prepare-for-emergencies/older-adults.html

How to prepare financially for a natural disaster. (2022). City National Bank. https:// www.cnb.com/personal-banking/insights/preparing-financially-for-natural- disaster.html

How to store water for drinking or cooking. (2021, September 1). Psu.edu. https:// extension.psu.edu/how-to-store-water-for-drinking-or-cooking

Hurricanes: Before, during, after. (2024). Red Cross Canada. https://www.redcross. ca/how-we-help/emergencies-and-disasters-in-canada/types-of-emergencies/

hurricanes

Igoe, K. J. (2017, July 24). *Emotional readiness and how to obtain it.* College Vine Blog. https://blog.collegevine.com/emotional-readiness-and-how-to-obtain-it#:

The importance of family emergency preparedness. (2019, September 19). Life Saver. https://iconlifesaver.com/news/the-importance-of-family-emergency-preparedness/. https://www.cdc.gov/orr/infographics/pfe-family.htm

The importance of first aid training | advanced consulting & training. (2022, February 22). Advanced Consulting and Training. https://advancedct.com/the-importance-of-first-aid-training/

Infographic: Prepare for everywhere - family preparedness. (2024). CDC

Jeff. (2019, November 22). *Self-sufficient living. how camping teaches us to be prepared.* My Knowledge Guy. https://www.myknowledgeguy.com/camping-teaches-preparedness/

Jeremy. (2022, April 4). *50 home safety tips and safety measures you can do this weekend.* Safety Talk Ideas. https://www.safetytalkideas.com/safety-tips/50-home-safety-tips-and-measures-you-can-do-this-weekend/

Keam, H. (2019, August 21). *Get to know your neighbors, they might just save your life.* Tamarackcommunity.ca. https://www.tamarackcommunity.ca/latest/get-to-know-your-neighbour-they-might-just-save-your-life

King James Bible. (2015). *Isaiah 43:2.* Bible Gateway. https://www.biblegateway.com/passage/?search=Isaiah%2043%3A2&version=KJV

King James Bible. (2018). *Galatians 6:9.* You Version the Bible App. https://www.bible.com/search/bible?query=Galatians%206%3A9

King James Bible. (2020). *1 Timothy 5:8.* BibleRef. https://www.bibleref.com/1-Timothy/5/1-Timothy-5-8.html

King James Bible. (2023a). *Ecclesiastes 7:12.* Bible Study Tools. https://www.biblestudytools.com/ecclesiastes/7-12.html

King James Bible. (2023b). *Proverbs 22:3.* Bible Study Tools. https://www.biblestudytools.com/proverbs/22-3.html#:

King James Bible. (2024a). *Genesis 41:36.* Bible Hub. https://biblehub.com/genesis/41-36.htm

King James Bible. (2024b). *Hebrews 10:24-25.* You Version the Bible App. https://www.bible.com/bible/1/HEB.10.24-25.KJV

King James Bible. (2024c). *Jeremiah 33:6.* Bible Hub. https://biblehub.com/jeremiah/33-6.htm

King James Bible. (2024d). *Luke 14:28-30.* You Version the Bible App. https://www.bible.com/bible/1/LUK.14.28-30.KJV

King James Bible. (2024e). *Proverbs 24:10.* You Version the Bible App. https://www.bible.com/bible/1/PRO.24.10.KJV

King James Bible. (2024f). *Psalm 127:1*. You Version the Bible App. https://www. bible.com/bible/1/PSA.127.1.KJV

Lisa. (2016, March 22). *Starting or joining a prepper group*. Survivalist Prepper. https://survivalistprepper.net/starting-or-joining-a-prepper-group/

Ma, H. (2022, October 6). *Why diversifying your income provides more opportunities in the long run*. StartupNation. https://startupnation.com/start-your-business/ why-diversifying-your-income-provides-more-opportunities-ma/

Mahatma Gandhi Quote: "The true measure of any society can be found in how it treats its most vulnerable members." (2024). Quotefancy. https://quotefancy.com/quote/ 856011/Mahatma-Gandhi-The-true-measure-of-any-society-can-be-found-in-how-it-treats-its-most

Making a family emergency plan. (2024). Marines.mil. https://www.ready. marines.mil/Make-a-Plan/Making-a-Family-Emergency-Plan/

Managing stress and building resilience - tips. (2022, March). Mind. https://www. mind.org.uk/information-support/types-of-mental-health-problems/stress/ managing-stress-and-building-resilience/

Marquardt, N., Stierle, K. E., van der Velden, E.-M., & Schürmann, V. (2023, June 28). *Mental readiness in emergency response tasks*. Research Gate. https://www. researchgate.net/publication/ 371938027_MENTAL_READINESS_IN_EMERGENCY_RESPONSE_ TASKS

Mayo Clinic Staff. (2022). *First-aid kits: Stock supplies that can save lives*. Mayo Clinic. https://www.mayoclinic.org/first-aid/first-aid-kits/basics/art-20056673

Monticello, A. (2021, March 10). *Are mobile homes safe? How to protect your camper from burglars*. The Home Security Superstore. https://www.thehomesecuritysu perstore.com/blogs/the-home-security-superstore-blog/are-mobile-homes-safe

Mountain House. (2020, April 30). *How to fit emergency planning into everyday life*. https://mountainhouse.com/blogs/emergency-prep-survival/emergency-plan ning-preparedness-everyday-life

National center for home food preservation. (2015). USDA Publications. https://nchfp. uga.edu/publications/publications_usda.html#gsc.tab=0%20and

Newman, K. M. (2016, November 9). *Five Science-Backed Strategies to Build Resilience*. Greater Good Magazine. https://greatergood.berkeley.edu/article/ item/five_science_backed_strategies_to_build_resilience

Nursetiawati, S., Siregar, J. S., & Josua, D. P. (2023). Understanding adaptability in the family environment in facing COVID-19. *Heliyon*, *9*(11), e20618–e20618. https://doi.org/10.1016/j.heliyon.2023.e20618

O'Shea, B., & Schwahn, L. (2016, October 4). *Budgeting 101: How to budget money.* NerdWallet. https://www.nerdwallet.com/article/finance/how-to-budget

Palupi, L., & Noor Rahman Himawan, M. (2020). A relationship between resilience and psychological preparedness for disaster among arranged university health faculty students. *E3S Web of Conferences, 202,* 12025. https://doi.org/10.1051/e3sconf/202020212025

Pangestu, D. (2024). *7 steps to saving money in an emergency fund.* My Money Coach. https://www.mymoneycoach.ca/blog/saving-emergency-fund.html

Pet safety in emergencies. (2024). CDC. https://www.cdc.gov/healthypets/keeping-pets-and-people-healthy/emergencies.html

Prepare your pets for disasters | ready.gov. (2023). Ready.gov. https://www.ready.gov/pets

Preparing emotionally for disasters and emergencies. (2024). Red Cross Canada. https://www.redcross.ca/how-we-help/emergencies-and-disasters-in-canada/be-ready-emergency-preparedness-and-recovery/preparing-emotionally-for-disasters-and-emergencies

Preparing for a hurricane or other tropical storm. (2024). https://www.cdc.gov/disasters/hurricanes/before.html

Public Safety Canada. (2022). *Emergency kits.* Getprepared.gc.ca. https://www.getprepared.gc.ca/cnt/kts/index-en.aspx

A quote by Mother Teresa. (2023). Goodreads. https://www.goodreads.com/quotes/63168-i-can-do-things-you-cannot-you-can-do-things

A quote by Warren Buffett. (n.d.). Goodreads. https://www.goodreads.com/quotes/7374491-do-not-save-what-is-left-after-spending-instead-spend

A quote by Winston S. Churchill. (n.d). Goodreads. https://www.goodreads.com/quotes/3270-success-is-not-final-failure-is-not-fatal-it-is

A quote from H.G Wells. (n.d.). BrainyQuote. https://www.brainyquote.com/citation/quotes/h_g_wells_121062

A quote from Hippocrates. (n.d.). BrainyQuotes. https://www.brainyquote.com/quotes/hippocrates_133222

A quote from Plato (n.d.). BrainyQuote. https://www.brainyquote.com/quotes/plato_110191

A quote from The Art of War. (n.d.). Goodreads. https://www.goodreads.com/quotes/608916-the-greatest-victory-is-that-which-requires-no-battle

Quotes from Will Durant. (n.d.). *We are what we repeatedly do. excellence, then, is not an act, but a habit.* BrainyQuote. https://www.brainyquote.com/quotes/will_durant_145967

Renner, M. (2024). *3 ways to stay positive in times of crisis.* Point Loma Nazarene University. https://www.pointloma.edu/resources/counseling-psychology/3-ways-stay-positive-times-crisis

Resilience – the key to overcoming natural disasters. (2019). Builders Project. https://buildersproject.eu/blog/post/3/resilience-the-key-to-overcome-natural-disasters

Responsible gun ownership: Ensuring safety through proper training and firearm handling. (2023, September 13). U.S. Law Shield. https://www.uslawshield.com/responsible-gun-ownership/

Richardson, J. (2023, September 5). *Disaster preparedness for older adults: A crucial consideration.* Tidal Basin Group. https://www.tidalbasingroup.com/disaster-preparedness-for-older-adults/

Ritter, J. (2024). *Involving children in childcare emergency preparedness.* Childcareaware.org. https://info.childcareaware.org/blog/involving-children-in-child-care-emergency-preparedness

Safety tips: Mobile homes. (2018). Miamidade.gov. https://www.miamidade.gov/global/fire/safety-mobile-homes.page

Sample childcare emergency action plan for training purposes only with multi-hazard planning for childcare. (2011). In *FEMA.* https://training.fema.gov/emiweb/is/is36/handouts%20-sample%20plans/eap_sample.pdf

Schlegelmilch, J. (2022, August 17). *Using budget principles to prepare for future disasters.* National Center for Disaster Preparedness | NCDP. https://ncdp.columbia.edu/ncdp-perspectives/using-budget-principles-to-prepare-for-future-pandemics-and-other-disasters/

Schwahn, L. (2017, May 17). *Zero-based budgeting: Spend every penny but meet your financial goals.* NerdWallet. https://www.nerdwallet.com/article/finance/zero-based-budgeting-explained

See, J. (2023, September 19). *How to prepare your home for a natural disaster.* Bankrate; Bankrate.com. https://www.bankrate.com/insurance/homeowners-insurance/natural-disaster-preparation/

7-habits-of-highly-resilient-families. (2017). Health hub. https://www.healthhub.sg/live-healthy/7-habits-of-highly-resilient-families

72-Hour kit checklist. (n.d.). https://www.wvc-ut.gov/DocumentCenter/View/9392/Emergency-Preparedness-Info

Steinkraus, K. H. (2024). *Lactic Acid Fermentations.* National Library of Medicine; National Academies Press (US). https://www.ncbi.nlm.nih.gov/books/NBK234703/

Sumra, H. (2019, August 21). *Home security tips for rural homes.* Smart Solutions for Home and Business. https://www.ooma.com/blog/home-security/home-security-tips-for-rural-homes/

Travels Risk Control. (2024). *Hurricane survival guide: What to do during and after the storm.* Travelers. https://www.travelers.com/resources/weather/hurricanes/hurricane-survival-guide

Troy. (2015, October 20). *DIY storage cabinets direct from the manufacturer*. Garage Cabinets. https://www.garagecabinets.com/gun-safety-101-how-to-store-guns-safely-in-your-home/

van Every, D. (2024). *Three ways for the entire family to have fun camping*. Nationalforests.org. https://www.nationalforests.org/blog/family-camping-tips

Vuković, D. (2022, October 21). *Survival food preservation: How to preserve food for long-term storage*. Primal Survivor. https://www.primalsurvivor.net/food-preservation-survivalists-guide/

Walter, E. (2024). *Know your neighbors - disaster response involves everyone*. Northcoast. coop. https://www.northcoast.coop/co-op_news/know-your-neighbors-disaster-response-involves-everyone

IMAGE REFERENCES

Acosta, A. (2021, January 27). *Assorted items o black surface*. [Image]. Pexels. https://www.pexels.com/photo/assorted-items-o-black-surface-6608038/

Alexey Demidov. (2022, June 14). *Water bottles on a wooden floor*. [Image]. Pexels. https://www.pexels.com/photo/water-bottles-on-a-wooden-floor-12496883/

Antranias. (2013). *Security lamps lantern*. [Image]. Pixabay. https://pixabay.com/photos/security-lamps-lantern-lighting-188201/

Barrett, R. (2023, April 21). *A shelf filled with containers and containers of food*. [Image]. Unsplash. https://unsplash.com/photos/a-shelf-filled-with-containers-and-containers-of-food-50HpEGK0YgY

Brown, R. (2020). *First aid and survival kits*. [Image]. Pexels. https://www.pexels.com/photo/first-aid-and-surival-kits-5125690/

Brown, R. (2020, September 23). *First aid tools*. [Image]. Pexels. https://www.pexels.com/photo/first-aid-tools-5146534/

Casetta, A. (2017, August 22). *Man, woman, and child walking together along dirt road*. [Image]. Unsplash. https://unsplash.com/photos/man-woman-and-child-walking-together-along-dirt-road-REKXJ7JhwiI

Dio Hasbi Saniskoro. (2019). *People doing group hand cheer*. [Image]. Pexels. https://www.pexels.com/photo/people-doing-group-hand-cheer-3280130/

Fauxels. (2019). Man wearing gray dress shirt and blue jeans. [Image]. Pexels. https://www.pexels.com/photo/man-wearing-gray-dress-shirt-and-blue-jeans-3184317/

Haupt, M. (2020, April). *White and blue plastic packs*. [Image]. Unsplash. https://unsplash.com/photos/white-and-blue-plastic-packs-WXnBzI7AypY

Jarmoluk. (2014). *Compote preserves jars*. [Image]. *Pixabay*. https://pixabay.com/photos/compote-preserves-jars-fruit-jam-428111/

Lumerman, D. (2018, January 29). *Car camping, getting ready for the great adventure in the outdoors, with supplies, coolers, food and clothing for the trip.* [Image]. Unsplash. https://unsplash.com/photos/Aexzy_P1wUs

Miroshnichenko, T. (2020, December 5). *Person in a shooting range.* [Image]. Pexels. https://www.pexels.com/photo/person-in-a-shooting-range-6092069/

Nerea Arance. (2022, April 19). *Bottles of Water.* [Image] Pexels. https://www.pexels.com/photo/bottles-of-water-11860560/

Nilov, M. (2021). *A couple looking at the laptop together* [Image]. Pexels. https://www.pexels.com/photo/a-couple-looking-at-the-laptop-together-6963026/

Splitt, M. (2021). *Man in gray long sleeve shirt and black pants sitting on brown wooden floor.* [Image]. Unsplash. https://unsplash.com/photos/man-in-gray-long-sleeve-shirt-and-black-pants-sitting-on-brown-wooden-floor-77-L2NUgWME

Stux. (2019). *Family hike travel.* [Image]. Pixabay. https://pixabay.com/photos/family-hike-travel-alps-4610864/

www.ingramcontent.com/pod-product-compliance
Lightning Source LLC
Chambersburg PA
CBHW070658130626
46553CB00005B/1763